MW00364878

MAJESTIC MOUNTAINS

Roaming the Great Mountain Ranges of Six Continents

Text and Photographs by

Leo Le Bon

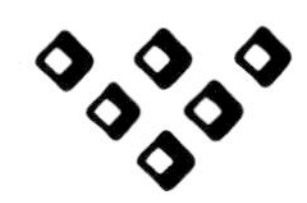

Thousands of tired, nerve shaken,
over-civilized people are beginning to find
out that going to the mountains is going home;
that wildness is a necessity; and that
mountain parks and reservations are useful not
only as fountains of lumber and irrigating
rivers, but as fountains of life.

—John Muir, *Our National Parks* (1901)

HARRY N. ABRAMS, INC., *Publishers*, NEW YORK

For the spirit of the mountains

page 1: Dent de Géant, Mt. Blanc Range, Alps, Italy/Switzerland
pages 2–3: Monument Valley, Utah/Arizona, U.S.A.
pages 4–5: Cuernos, Cordillera Paine, Patagonia, Chile
pages 6–7: Panorama of the Alps, Italy/Switzerland
pages 8–9: South face of Kilimanjaro, Tanzania
pages 10–11: Minya Konka, Hengduan Mountains, China
page 12: Tre Cime di Lavaredo, Dolomites, Italy
Above: Near the Matterhorn, Italy
pages 16–17: The Alps, Italy

Editor: Lois Brown

Designer: Dirk Luykx

Library of Congress Cataloging-in-Publication Data
Le Bon, Leo.
Majestic mountains: roaming the great mountain ranges of six continents with Leo Le Bon/Leo Le Bon.
p. cm.
Bibliography: p. 214
ISBN 0-8109-1539-1
1. Photography of mountains. 2. Le Bon, Leo. I. Title
TR787.L42 1989
779'.36'0924—dc19

Published in 1989 by Harry N. Abrams, Incorporated, New York

A Times Mirror Company

Printed in Italy

CONTENTS

PREFACE

I am the seeker, the "Mountain Quester" who ranges across the mountains of the world. I am reaching for that which man seeks . . . call it what you will, the essence of life, wisdom, peace, fulfillment. I have wandered the world in modern-day fashion, seeing more in 30 years of jetting the planet than Thomas Mann could imagine would be possible in ten lifetimes when he wrote his immortal novel, *The Magic Mountain*, more than 60 years ago.

Mountain questing, rather than mountain-eering . . . the questing, like the climbing, is not just a noble profession but a way of life. This may place me in the guileless fools class,

unspoiled still by civilization. Yet what *have* I seen in these 30 years? Some people think that because I have traveled so much, my life would seem so long. But it's just the opposite—my life has flashed by—I don't remember anything. It's the opposite of the wretched jailbird whose sentence appears so interminably long because he is deprived of all sensory perception. To remember these mountain moments, I take photographs—they are my passion, my solace, my lifesaver. I cling to those two-dimensional images of celluloid as if they were the sublimation, the substitution for the adventurous quest into the mystery of life. I think that Thomas Mann would have understood.

Berkeley
August 1988

NORTH AMERICA

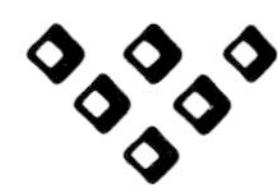

Early one fall, I made a climb on Half Dome in Yosemite. The changing colors were at their best and the leaves had started piling up along the meadows. Big, dark clouds were furling high in the sky, giving the sheer granite walls the deep blue haze of oncoming winter. The air was crisp and crystal clear, and from high up on Half Dome I could see the sun shooting a thousand shafts of light into the river 4,000 feet below. As the light splattered on the water, it was as if suddenly my mind opened and I became essential matter. I no longer existed—rock, earth, and mountains around me became spiritual and suspended. The only objects which remained unchanged were the cars, driving along the meadow in the far distance below me. Life became the one and only essence . . . the occasional whining of the wind along the mountain face, the light streaking across the granite walls. The warming rays of the sun played hide and seek among the clouds and when they touched me, they urged me forward. I climbed higher, stretched for the next solution hold, a few more inches, and I reached a ledge. I no longer saw the rock, the mountains, nor the curving ripple of crystals we were climbing along Half Dome's neck. I only saw colors, lines, forms, rhythms, silhouettes, dimensions, movements, happenings . . . then no longer even that . . . only it. I was no longer . . . I went with it. I was now everywhere, suspended, and nowhere. My body reached the top and wandered among the peaks, but my mind had been set free.

Half Dome, Yosemite, California

Overleaf: Mt. Shasta, California

Many years later, I found myself on Mt. Shasta in northern California. It was dark and cold. The alarm clock had gone off and I'd gotten up. I was camped at Panther Meadows with my two grown children, Suzanne and William. It had been more than ten years since we'd been together in the mountains. Alas, time passes quickly . . . high school, exams, college, social life, dating—no more time for family trips into the Sierras. Then one day, just as luck would have it, we were together with a free weekend on our hands and we agreed to go climb a mountain, deciding on Shasta, a seven-hour drive from our home in Berkeley, California.

In preparation for the climb, I organized the gear and packed up, but they were still in their sleeping bags. "Come on, guys," I urged them, "the mountain is waiting!" Half an hour later we were on our way, Bill and I sharing a flashlight that worked intermittently. The pre-dawn start-up on a big mountain is always magical. The soft howling of the wind, the labored breathing of my companions, and the looming presence of the enormous, invisible mountain above combine to convey a feeling of mystery. When at last the black sky begins to pale, the light gives birth to ridges, slopes of rock, and fields of snow . . . the magic begins. Slowly the curtain opens and the earth's greatest show—a grand sunrise and a new day—begins anew.

The first rays of the sun flashing over the eastern horizon in the far distance cast our mountain in perspective. We again took on our true identity: there was Sue's yellow parka, and Bill's ski jacket was as brilliantly red as I remembered it just yesterday. The transition of night into day was now behind us; we moved steadily up, traversing from the Green Butte ridge into Avalanche Gulch, the standard route on Shasta's south side. Clambering across

loose shale and gray pumice, we reached a small promontory overlooking a bluff, where on a small, level camping area near the shores of Lake Helen, I counted four pitched tents, but there was no one around yet. As we quietly moved higher up the mountain, we reached the snow line. An icy gully choked with large boulders and glistening icicles led up for hundreds of feet toward a vast expanse of snow and a rocky island known as the Heart. It then veered right only to dissipate into a long, steep, and interminable slope of mixed snow and scree to the Red Banks. The Banks appeared above us: a bright-orange wall of rotten volcanic lava etched stunningly against the snow. This is the magic of big mountains—the light, the coloring, the intensity of the images, the shapes of ridges, the snowfields, the ice pinnacles, the hoar frost on the red rock. Shasta has all this—a fairy garden reaching into the sky. Up here I felt like becoming part of the mountain. Then suddenly we reached the crest of the Red Banks, with time for a rest and breakfast. Bill had been quiet while working his way up steadily and effortlessly, climbing with balanced grace. Suzy had stayed behind me; she had been feeling apprehensive and felt more secure closer to me. Now past the moderate difficulties, we trudged up Misery Hill and arrived at the summit plateau. Covered with three-foot-tall "nieves penitentes" (vertical ice pinnacles caused by uneven melting of an old snowfield), the pinnacles marred a quick traverse to the top. Stepping and stumbling over and across this football-sized field of "snow-cicles," we finally reached the rocky summit pyramid and, ten minutes later, stood on the top. There, in the thin, clear air and the glaring sunlight, we joyfully embraced and rejoiced in our success. We also learned anew to know ourselves for what we are and to assess our individual capabilities. But best of all, we renewed the bonds of trust and friendship between a father and his adult children, grown apart by the inevitable forces of time and distance.

Summit plateau of Mt. Shasta

Opposite above: Mt. Athabasca, Canadian Rockies

Opposite below: View from the Trans-Canada Highway in the Canadian Rockies

Totem Pole and Yei-Bichei Formation
in Monument Valley, Utah/Arizona

One might well ask: what is mountain climbing, and how does one differentiate between the various activities such as high-altitude backpacking, scrambling, "peak-bagging," rock-climbing, technical mountaineering—or alpinism—and expeditionary climbing, all of which come under the general term "climbing"? While the latest generation of "hot-shot" gymnasts test their mettle on the sheer rock faces of El Capitan or Half Dome in Yosemite, others are backpacking across some tough 13,000-foot pass in the Rockies. Still others are peak-bagging, which means scrambling up any mountain, usually by the easiest route mainly to add that mountain to one's list of climbs. Mt. Shasta in northern California is such a peak, technically easy by the standard route but a long and strenuous haul nevertheless. More serious climbing is to be had on technically difficult peaks with hard routes on walls and steep ridges of snow and ice, requiring experience and skill in the use of climbing equipment such as rope, pitons, crampons, and an ice axe. The pleasure of climbing a mountain is derived from the struggle to overcome difficulties—be they technical or otherwise. Steep rock-climbing can produce a natural high just as readily as a long slog up an interminable snow slope.

Generally speaking, most mountains in the continental United States are rock peaks, with the more difficult snow and ice mountains to be found in Canada and Alaska. In terms of scenery, variety of terrain, and climbing opportunities, the mountains of North America have it all: world-class rock climbing in Yosemite; excellent mountaineering in the Rockies, Sierra Nevada, Tetons, Wind Rivers, and more; high altitude snow and ice climbing on the giant volcanoes of Mexico as well as on those of our own Northwest; and desert climbing on the stunning sandstone towers in Arizona and Utah. Moreover, there are endless possibilities of technically demanding climbs in the Canadian Rockies and the Coastal Ranges, not to mention the big ice climbs of Alaska. And although some areas are occasionally congested, such as Yosemite in late spring and early fall and the Tetons during summer, there are other opportunities for climbers, backpackers, and mountain-wanderers to travel to their heart's content among the ranges of North America.

Monument Valley

During the past 30 years, I have spent most of my climbing weekends in the Sierra Nevada, a magnificent wilderness of high meadows, blue lakes, granite peaks, waterfalls, and summer snowfields, and in the Yosemite Valley, where hundreds of difficult rock-climbing routes require advanced technical skills, endurance, and a cool head to prevail over the terrifying exposure of the big walls. In the High Sierra, the peaks have moderate approaches and usually a "normal" route or scramble to get to the top. The same can be said for the Rocky Mountains. Mt. Whitney, the highest peak in the continental United States, is a good example of a non-technical peak that can be climbed in one or two days along the regular route (which, in fact, is a trail). All that is required is a good pair of shoes, camping gear, and a

Yosemite Valley in winter

steady companion. Climbing in North America is generally more relaxed, more casual, and less "obsessive" than the way Europeans climb in the Alps. Generally speaking, Americans and Canadians tend to go about climbing their mountains not with a sense of urgency but with a feeling of "being in touch" with nature. Most climbing parties bring all their gear and food with them—few are the peaks that do not require camping or backpacking, and huts are rare or nonexistent. This style of mountaineering is, if not typical, at least the most common way of "going climbing" in North America.

Mt. Assiniboine

Canadian Rockies, British Columbia, Canada

The eastern ramparts of the Canadian Rockies are a fortresslike wall featuring peaks of exceptional beauty. The casual visitor who drives west from Calgary along Trans-Canada Highway 1 to the town of Banff, and further along the famous Icefield Parkway from Lake Louise to the town of Jasper, will enjoy unending displays of snow-clad peaks, hanging glaciers, huge icefields, and emerald-colored alpine lakes. Yet the spectacle from Highway 1 and the Icefield Parkway is mere foreplay, a castellated mountain facade, when compared with what lies beyond the road along and across the Continental Divide to the west.

Just 25 miles south of Banff, at the southern edge of one of British Columbia's smaller provincial parks, rises one of the Rockies' shapeliest peaks, Mt. Assiniboine (11,870′), the "Matterhorn of Canada." A near-perfect pyramid of decaying limestone, the mountain was first seen in 1884 by Canadian geologist George Dawson from the summit of Copper Mountain. The following year Dawson named the peak after the Assiniboine Indians, a former Sioux tribe that migrated into the Rockies and made the area near the mountain their hunting grounds.

Although five peaks in the Rockies are higher than Assiniboine—among them Mt. Robson (12,972′), "king" of the Rockies and the highest, and Mt. Columbia (12,392′), which stands sentinel above the vast glaciers of the Columbia Icecap—none are more awe-inspiring than Assiniboine, whose formidable wedge towers almost 5,000 feet into the sky above Lake Magog (7,005′), lying at the foot of the dramatic V-shaped cirque of peaks neighboring Assiniboine.

Mt. Assiniboine

Overleaf: Mt. Assiniboine and frozen Lake Magog

Boreal forests of spruce, lodgepole pine, and alpine fir flourish here along with hundreds of species of wildflowers that bloom in midsummer. Snow covers the high peaks year-round and remains at the lower levels until early summer. The land around Assiniboine is home to a surprising variety of wildlife: moose, deer, Rocky Mountain goat, elk, bighorn sheep, coyote, wolf, and grizzly have been observed, while lynx, cougar, and wolverine are rare visitors.

Assiniboine was first climbed by Sir James Outram and party on September 3, 1901. Their route took them up the southwest face and down by the north ridge (now the standard route). Edward Whymper, the conqueror of the Swiss Matterhorn, visited Assiniboine the same year but did not take part in the attempt to ascend it. Perhaps he abstained from the climb because of his age—he was 62. Dr. Tom Longstaff made the first ascent of the northwest face in 1910, a moderate route except for a steep, holdless 60-foot wall that Longstaff overcame with difficulty:

> About noon we stood at the foot of the final cliff. . . . We both feared that we were beaten. There was no other possible alternative but to go straight up and for the first ten or twelve feet there was no handhold. Rudolf tried in two places but had to give up: he was too heavy to use me as a ladder. Retreat was suggested; but I was terrified of the prospect of descending our icy stairway and preferred to try the cliff myself. I climbed on to Rudolf's shoulders and then on to his head. At last I

The Assiniboine Lodge

managed to find a fair hold, and prodded from below by Rudolf's ice-axe I made a few feet. Digging the tips of my fingers into minute cracks or on to tiny horizontal edges, by main force I clawed my way up inch by inch. The cracks in the rock were full of ice; once, losing sensation in my finger-tips, I almost fell backwards. Sheer necessity compelled me to cling on. Rudolf had a good stance below, but it was a horrid drop, and the ice slopes we had ascended looked terrifying in perspective. Only the utmost concentration of willpower enabled me to get up the first thirty feet; then I was able to jam my thigh sideways into an incipient chimney and ease the strain. I have never climbed by sheer mental effort before nor since. The next twenty feet were only very difficult; a matter of just forcing a way up inch by inch and making no mistake.

The direct north- and east-face routes on the peak are undoubtedly the hardest to climb. The north face was conquered in 1967 by Yvon Chouinard, Joe Faint, and Chris Jones; the east face was climbed in 1969 by Bill Davidson and Archie Simpson. Nowadays, beginning at the Assiniboine Lodge, located near Lake Magog, the mountain is usually climbed in about 12 hours via the mostly fourth-class north ridge.

In 1922 the scenic area north of the mountain was declared a provincial park under the instigation of Arthur Wheeler, a pioneer surveyor of the Rockies and a prominent member of the prestigious Canadian Alpine Club. Wheeler built a cabin near Lake Magog to which he brought hikers on his then famous "150-mile walking tours" from Banff. In 1927 Erling Strom and a group of adventurers skied into the Assiniboine area and stayed at Wheeler's cabin. On his return to the East Coast, Strom persuaded the barons of the Canadian Pacific Railroad to construct a comfortable lodge near the mountain. The thinking at the time was that the CPR would build a string of hotels along the track to attract additional train passengers. A beginning had been made in 1888 with the opening of the Banff Springs Hotel, billed at the time as "the finest hotel on the North American continent," and in 1890 with the building of a small "chateau" at Lake Louise. People could now take the train to a luxury hotel in the middle of an incredible and virtually unexplored wilderness and climb unnamed and unclimbed peaks at random. The lodge at Assiniboine was built in the summer of 1928 and Strom became caretaker, a job he held for 50 years! The Assiniboine lodge is now a historic site and the present concession holders have renovated and considerably upgraded the facilities.

Cross-country skiers on Mt. Assiniboine's Wonder Pass

Mt. Shasta

Cascade Range, California, U.S.A.

Mt. Shasta is *the* king-sized mountain that dominates northern California, surging to a height of 14,162 feet. A dormant volcano and part of the Cascade Range, Shasta's slopes of volcanic ash and pumice rise 7,000 feet above treeline. The northern and eastern slopes are buried by five good-sized glaciers, of which the Whitney Glacier is the largest (and also the largest in California). It was Clarence King, author of *Mountaineering in the Sierra Nevada*, published in 1872 and a classic in its time, who first discovered the existence of the Shasta glaciers during his climb of the peak in 1870. Until that time, it was generally believed that no glaciers of any substance existed in California.

Mt. Shasta

Mt. Shasta was first seen by explorer Peter Ogden in 1827, but not climbed until 27 years later—by the manager of a local sawmill, E. D. Pearce, in 1854. Coincidentally, the year 1854 also marks the first ascents of other Cascade giants: Mt. Hood and Mt. Adams. Pearce climbed the mountain by way of a broad avalanche ravine on the west side of Shasta, which remains to this day the standard route up the peak.

In 1922 the Sierra Club acquired 80 acres of virgin fir forest along the western treeline, below Pearce's route, and there built a small, one-room stone lodge commonly known as Horse Camp (7,900′). Mac Olberman was the first custodian to be appointed and remained actively involved in the management of the club's property into his 70th year, when he was still able to climb the peak in slightly over five hours, an excellent time. Years later the club purchased an additional 640 acres, and today the well-maintained hut is used by a large number of climbers and hikers, as well as ski mountaineers and cross-country tourers.

To the first-time visitor who drives up Interstate 5, Shasta is an impressive sight. During winter and spring the mountain dons its glorious white mantle of snow and looks truly stunning from afar—its enormous bulk etched white against the blue California sky, rising out of green forested foothills like a gigantic frosted iceberg. In late summer and fall, however, when most of the snow has melted and the slopes look blotched and barren, none of the five glaciers are visible from the west. Only one feature stands out, a large orange-red pumice band at 12,600 feet—clearly visible from the town of Mt. Shasta, 9,000 feet below—known as the Red Banks. Shasta's summit is not visible from the town as it is hidden behind Misery Hill, a 1,500-foot ridge that leads to the upper plateau and was so named when it was found the summit was still some way to go. A more redeeming image of Shasta can be had by driving along U.S. Highway 97, from where four of Shasta's glaciers can be seen.

Shasta is very much a climber's mountain, attracting mountaineers from all over California, Oregon, Washington, and beyond. The peak can be climbed year-round, offering many challenging routes to the beginner as well as to the seasoned

The lower slopes of Mt. Shasta

Sierra Club hut
on Mt. Shasta

mountaineer. In winter and spring there is the added attraction of superb ski mountaineering along Shasta's many broad gulches, open slopes, and bowls.

As mentioned, the peak is most often climbed from the west along Pearce's original route, due partially to easy access by car from the town of Mt. Shasta along the Everett Memorial Highway, which takes climbers up to the 7,000-foot level at Bunny Flat, or beyond to Panther Meadows. This road was originally constructed to service the now-defunct Shasta ski area but remains plowed all winter. The standard route, known as Avalanche Gulch, starts from near here and passes by the Sierra Club's hut, where overnight accommodations are available in bunks (bring your sleeping bag). From here an elaborate stone trail, known as Olberman's Causeway, leads upward to the Gulch and disappears below tiny Helen Lake (10,400′). Beyond this small pond is a formation known as the Heart, and above it to the right are the Red Banks. This is the most popular and perhaps quickest way up Shasta and is not technically difficult. Yet, according to statistics, only 50% of the starters reach the top, the total elevation gain from the road being more than 7,000 vertical feet over a distance of 4.1 miles—in actuality a brutal piece of exercise for anyone not in excellent shape. In addition, Shasta is reputed to make its own weather, often of the hurricane variety, making ascents sometimes dangerous and even impossible. For this reason many climbers prefer to spend the night at Helen Lake, where several rock platforms have been laid out by countless previous parties. From the lake it takes less than five hours to reach the top, up along the 35° slopes of the Heart to the foot of the Red Banks. This impressive-looking wall can be surmounted easily by climbing a narrow chute at the base (in summer) or around to the right (best in winter). From the top of the Banks, one trudges up Misery Hill toward the summit plateau. Near the base of the final 150-foot summit rock is an active sulphur spring, proving that while Shasta might no longer be active, perhaps it merely remains in a dormant state for the time being. John Muir, the first president of the Sierra Club and a great naturalist, climbed Shasta in 1875 and bivouacked by these hot springs during a blizzard. He later described these fumaroles as "the last feeble expression of the mighty forces that built the mountain."

From the summit there are spectacular views of northern California, including the Trinity Alps, Mt. Lassen, the Marble Mountains, and the nearby Castle Crags.

Half Dome

Yosemite, Sierra Nevada, California, U.S.A.

Within the Sierra Nevada of California lies the incomparable Yosemite Valley, with its sheer 3,000-foot granite walls, waterfalls, meandering streams, and sparkling lakes. At the east end of the valley rises Yosemite's most majestic rock formation, Half Dome (8,842′), an enormous granite mass uplifted during a geological intrusion millions of years ago and later worn down by glaciation and exfoliation. Nearly a vertical mile above the valley sprawls the high country, the "range of light" of John Muir. All this is part of Yosemite National Park, the crown jewel in the diadem of American parklands. It is a 1,200-square-mile geological wonderland, enclosing the finest mountain scenery of the 300-mile-long Sierra Nevada of California.

The first white man to lay eyes on this incomparable valley was Joseph Walker, an adventurous woodsman who encountered Yosemite in 1833 after a three-month overland trek from Wyoming. It was not from the valley floor that he gaped in awe at what he saw, but from 3,000 feet above on the upper rim of the valley. Walker, a contemporary of Kit Carson (and according to his biographer, Bill Gilbert, "an idol to John Frémont"), was unable to find his way down—the cliffs were impossible to descend and he could see no route between them.

The floor of the valley, which lies at approximately a 4,000-foot elevation, was visited for the first time in 1851, when members of the mounted Mariposa Battalion pursued a band of Indians, members of the Miwok tribe, into their remote sanctuary. The battalion easily overpowered the Indians and their chief, Tenaya. The entire tribe, who called themselves Ahwahneechee (deep grassy valley), was taken prisoner and exiled to a reservation near the present city of Fresno, California. Studies have since revealed that these Indians had made their home in the valley for more than 4,000 years!

Merced River in Yosemite Valley

Overleaf: Winter sunset on Half Dome

Soon after the events of 1851, Yosemite Valley became a major tourist attraction in the West. One of the early visitors was Thomas Ayers, who made sketches of the valley and in 1856 published the first pictures of Half Dome and other important landmarks in *California* magazine. In 1864 President Lincoln signed an Act of Congress granting the area to California "for public use . . . inalienable for all time."

In 1869 James Hutchings attempted to climb Half Dome but could not find his way beyond the saddle on the east side of the upper dome. Around the same time John Muir visited Yosemite Valley, attracted in part by the magnificent scenery and the wide-open wilderness of the high country above. He wrote eloquently of the need for conserving the outstanding scenic and wild areas. His efforts influenced Congress, which established the present boundaries of the park in 1890. (Muir, by the way, was also the first to theorize that Yosemite was formed by glaciation, a controversial proposition at the time.)

Half Dome was eventually climbed by George Anderson in October 1875. By drilling holes in the granite, into which he then inserted iron spikes, he laboriously worked his way to the top along the east face, now the standard route of ascent. Anderson's spikes have long since been replaced with steel cables and wooden steps, so that almost anyone can climb to the top of this amazing dome and look down its northwest face, a wall sliced smooth by glaciers some 10,000 years ago.

Left: Yosemite Falls

Above: View from Yosemite's Dewey Point

Opposite:
Don Lauria and
Dennis Henneck
on the second ascent
of El Capitan's North
America Wall

The first ascent of the impressive 2,000-foot northwest face (the sheer wall seen by tourists in the valley) was made in 1957 by Royal Robbins, Jerry Gallwas, and Mike Sherrick in an epic five-day assault. The climb became the first Grade VI in America (a Grade VI is the hardest overall grade or classification given to multiday rock climbs in the United States) and is regarded as one of the great classic American rock climbs—attempted annually by a large number of American as well as foreign expert climbers.

In addition to the above routes, Half Dome has endured the trauma of countless other ascents hammered out on its smooth granite walls. Among these is the "Tis-sa-ack" (named after dark streaks on the wall supposedly formed by tears of the Indian maiden Tis-sa-ack, shed for a fallen lover), which required no less than 110 expansion bolts to be placed. The south face route on Half Dome is also worthy of mention, as the route required six attempts over several years before yielding to the "mad bolters" who drilled at minimum 180 steel pins into the rock. Last, but not least, is a superb and popular route called "Snake Dike," first done by a party of Yosemite "resident" climbers who in 1965 discovered a subtle quartz dike on the southwest face. This route, entirely free of artificial aids, is climbed along the small protuberances of the one-foot-wide dike.

While up on the walls, the climbers reign supreme in their exalted state; down in the valley it's like being in Los Angeles. Yosemite is overcrowded beyond belief during the summer—buses, cars, and trucks are parked everywhere; campgrounds are overflowing; trails are crowded with people and bicycles; long lines are to be found at all food concessions; and souvenir shops are filled with junk and pseudo-Indian artifacts. The once serene oasis known to Muir and Hutchings—and the Indians before them—has been nearly obliterated. The only sane time for a visit is between seasons, or perhaps during a storm, when the valley is transformed into a magical stage with clouds swirling past the high glistening walls and lightning striking the granite domes and spires in an eerie display of nature's grandest spectacle.

Totem Pole

Colorado Plateau, Arizona, U.S.A.

Monument Valley, which belongs to the Colorado Plateau uplift, straddles the Arizona-Utah border near Four Corners, the only place in the United States where four states meet (Arizona, Utah, New Mexico, and Colorado). Here red sandstone, displaying hues from salmon pink to fiery burnt carmine, creates spatial towers that seem to float over measureless distances, producing vistas of incredible beauty and grandeur. This valley, part of the great American southwestern desert also known as "Indian Country," is perhaps one of the most scenic yet least known of our national treasures. Weldon Heald described Monument Valley in a superb essay in Roderick Peattie's book *The Inverted Mountains:* "Monument Valley is not beautiful. It is too vast, too silent, too empty to touch any human response in us save that of awe. Its effect is as if the aspiring obelisks, giant tombs, and wasting towers were the ruins of some gargantuan forgotten city of which even the memory of its inhabitants has been lost in the mists of time."

One of the valley's most spectacular landmarks is the Totem Pole, a slender (only 20 feet in diameter), 500-foot-high spire of red sandstone. The top is flat, large enough to just fit a desk, a chair, and an IBM typewriter—exactly what a television commercial depicted several years ago. All the equipment was lifted to the top by helicopter, including the "secretary," Carrie Cullin, who volunteered for the job.

First climbed in 1957 by a team of daring Californians—William "Dolt" Feuerer, Mark Powell, Don Wilson, and Jerry Gallwas—the Pole today is strictly out of bounds to rock climbers. Not only is it sacred to the Navajos—part of a formation called Yei-Bichei (supernatural beings after which a Navajo firedance is also named) that stands on Navajo ancestral hunting grounds and the present reservation—but conservationists fear that a climber's iron pitons and expansion bolts will shorten the life expectancy of the spire.

Totem Pole

Monument Valley can easily be reached from the nearest airport, which is in Flagstaff, Arizona. Driving northeast along Highway 160, then north through Kayenta, the traveler crests a subtle divide and suddenly enters Monument Valley. The first formations that come into view are the spectacular Agathlan, climbed in 1949 with a forced overnight on a ledge below the summit, and famed Owl Rock, both distinct landmarks. Beyond lies the vast expanse of the valley floor studded with innumerable mesas, towers, pinnacles, and half-formed arches—a land of such deceptive size and proportions that it prompted Zane Grey to characterize it as "a yellow-and-purple corrugated world of distance."

Monument Valley is sparsely vegetated: sagebrush, scrub juniper, and pinyon pine are the few plants that can subsist without much water (only eight inches of rainfall a year) under the merciless sun. About halfway across the valley is a turnoff leading west to Old Baldy Mesa and the site of another valley landmark, Goulding's Trading Post. Harry Goulding came to Monument Valley in 1922 as a young shepherd, became one of its better guides, then brought along his wife, "Mike," and set up shop near Old Baldy. Today, the Gouldings' store is a tourist attraction of its own, selling genuine Navajo jewelry, wedding baskets, and blankets, as well as the usual tourist souvenirs.

Historically, the area around Monument Valley has a fascinating past and is rich in archaeological treasures. Many interesting sites can be visited, such as Keet Seel, Betatakin, Inscription House, and scores of smaller cliff dwellings—all part of the Navajo National Monument. Most of these sites were the homes of the Anasazi, who are believed to have lived in this area as early as 600 A.D.

The mountains and natural formations surrounding Monument Valley and Four Corners represent landmarks not only to the rock climber and to the intrepid trekker who travels cross-country in search of space and solitude but also to the casual tourist, who in many instances can enjoy the spectacular sites from the car window. Some of these landmarks include Shiprock, a huge volcanic plug in northwest New Mexico, first climbed by David Brower and friends in 1939; Navajo Mountain, the most sacred of all the peaks to the Navajo, overlooking famed Rainbow Bridge (which can now be approached by boat from Lake Powell); and Spider Rock, an 800-foot-tall spire, the highest freestanding rock pinnacle in America, located in glorious Canyon de Chelly National Monument. All of these unique southwest mountains, monuments, and natural arches are located south of the Colorado and San Juan rivers, the natural boundary of the Navajo Indian Reservation, one of the largest in America.

To approach the Totem Pole, continue from Goulding's to Navajo Tribal Park, in the center of Monument Valley (an area approximately 5 miles wide by 14 miles long) and drive along the loop road to its easternmost end. The Pole, which desert climber Steve Roper described as "a fearsome red shaft, so thin and precariously built that the thought of climbing it sends shudders through the body," can then be reached by walking a short distance across undulating sand dunes and then contemplated up close with a generous dose of good, old-fashioned awe.

Monument Valley

Opposite:
Rainbow Bridge in Utah

Overleaf:
Goosenecks of the
San Juan, Utah

SOUTH AMERICA

No single, major mountain chain dominates the landscape of a continent as does the Andes in South America. Known by their full name as "Cordillera de los Andes," these mountains run in a practically unbroken chain from near the Panama Canal to Cape Horn, a distance of over 4,500 miles. Along this vast distance (the range is not a uniform and unbroken barrier of high peaks), there are many subranges of great beauty and breathtaking peaks, as well as convoluted ridges, nondescript hilly terrain, isolated volcanoes, and miscellaneous transverse ranges of minor importance. But, on the whole, the Andes form a total watershed between the great pampa of Argentina and the vast Mato Grosso jungles of Brazil to the east, and the mountainous and hilly lands of Colombia, Ecuador, Peru, and Chile to the west.

Yerupajá, Cordillera Huayhuash, Peru

Among the more important of these smaller ranges that comprise the great Andes is the spectacular Cordillera Blanca of Peru. A close second are the granite spires of Fitzroy and Paine along the Chilean-Argentine border in Patagonia. The monarch of the entire range is Aconcagua, highest mountain of the Western Hemisphere, a popular peak with American and European climbers alike. Yet Aconcagua is a treacherous mountain, having taken many lives of unaware climbers not prepared for its fierce, unpredictable storms and high altitude. Although not particularly attractive, Aconcagua is nevertheless a worthwhile objective for those willing to undergo the hardships of climbing above 22,000 feet, suffering oxygen deprivation, cold, and exhaustion. Those at highest risk are people with little or no climbing experience who believe the mountain is a mere walk-up and who are unfamiliar with the potential dangers.

Summit ridge of Aconcagua (south face on the right), Argentina

After spending a night at the Plantamura Refuge at 20,000 feet on Aconcagua, I experienced a wide variety of thoughts on awakening the following morning. A knock on the door and a loud voice outside the tiny hut activated my numbed mind and consciousness surged slowly from a bottomless, soundless whirlpool. As I lay bundled up in my sleeping bag, a sullen, insipid pain began to creep up my spine. Ten hours of agitated, uneven sleep had not erased the exertion to get here. Everything ached. The outside air was wafting in, and it was thin, raw, and icy cold. Where was I? Then I suddenly knew . . . on Aconcagua . . . 20,000 feet up, and this was to be our summit day. A sudden rebellion welled up inside me; how do I get up? Where are my glasses? My flashlight? What time is it? What is the weather like? Where on earth are my boots? Is anyone else awake yet? I needed to get up and melt snow for drinking water and prepare food. Seemingly endless data rushed across my mind. As if helped by an unseen hand, I sat up. Suddenly I rejoiced. This would be a fantastic day, and I was living just the first few minutes of it. My heart was pounding, and my head was dizzy from the altitude and the euphoria. Would we make it to the summit? An immediate fear clamped my chest. I tried not to think in this vein and forced myself to ignore any thought of failure. But the thoughts came back—it was a continuous struggle. While I dressed, I had a vision of sitting on a litter-covered beach, with shreds of cloth, paper, and bits of old plastic sheeting being blown up by the offshore wind. I tried to fight off these images—I wanted to see the blue water, touch the warm sand, feel the sunshine, hear the gulls. Then the garbage and the beach disappeared. I continued to struggle with my frozen leather boots, ignoring the pain in my back and the oppression in my chest while I tried to lace them. Why was it so difficult? At last I could sit up, recover, and take deep breaths. With a grasping urge, I groped in the dark for the trapdoor, stumbled outside, and staggered to my feet. I looked around . . . it was still pitch dark, but the three small huts were visible: Berlin, Libertad, and Plantamura. I had come out just in time, for a streak of light then appeared between dark clouds. The moment of dawn was near. Aconcagua was frightfully ugly—gray volcanic ash and pumice were all around, and except for a few snowpatches, the whole north face of the mountain was one gigantic rubble heap of eroded rock towers, scattered boulders, scree, and dirty, yellowish sulphur powder. Despite a heavy down jacket, shivers ran through my entire body.

We spent a miserable hour melting water and fumbling with breakfast. Our stomachs refused to cooperate. Then the moment of action arrived. As we left the mess hut, the miracle of the new day was with us. The summit was afire with a deep red, and the warmth of the sun's first rays filled me with an immense satisfaction. Taking my first steps towards the summit, I entered a silent symphony, hearing only this verse from the *Rubaiyat*:

> Awake! for morn in the bowl of night
> has cast the stone that puts the stars to flight
> and lo! The warrior of the East has caught
> the Sultan's turret in a noose of light.

The strongest were soon gone, disappearing behind boulders and ridges that intersected the 3,000-foot-high north face. Toward midday I reached the traverse that is the final gully leading to the summit—the infamous "*canaleta*," a 250-foot-long chute filled with large boulders teetering precariously on soft sandlike pumice. While four of us were tackling this last obstacle, one of the climbers, John, complained of a severe headache and was unable to continue. Fearing that John had contracted cerebral edema, I decided to abort the final push for the summit and take him down the mountain. Staggering out of control, John barely managed to stay on his feet. Slowly we made our way out of the "death zone" to around 22,000 feet. Here John sagged to the ground and I sat down with him. When—what seemed just a moment later—I woke up from a cat nap, John had disappeared. I climbed down a stretch of mountain in search of him, but he was nowhere to be found. He simply had vanished!

Frantically I tried to cover the huge expanse of the north face of this enormous mountain but without success. My yelling and yodeling for John was answered only by the wind. He must have headed down while I dozed, I thought; perhaps I had slept longer than just a few moments. Eventually I reached the Plantamura hut, praying he would be there. I found only Jeff. We immediately began a rescue effort. Jeff organized a search party that soon disappeared into the gathering darkness.

The night was long. As dawn struck the mountain, I saw Jeff and John and the rest of the team coming down from the upper reaches of Aconcagua—safe and sound. John simply had started walking down the mountain while I slept. He tripped and fell out of sight behind a boulder. Upon recovering consciousness, he staggered down the mountain until he was found by the rescue party. A harrowing experience above 20,000 feet—but a happy ending.

Left: Honda Valley,
Cordillera Blanca,
Peru

Below: Jirishanca,
Cordillera Huayhuash,
Peru

Right: Huascarán,
Cordillera Blanca,
Peru

Below: Volcano Licancábur,
Atacama Desert,
Chilean Andes,
Chile

Interesting and desirable mountains to climb need not always be high. On the contrary, smaller peaks where altitude and frigid air are not contributing factors are often much more enjoyable. Lower peaks are usually less remote and thus have easier access. In southern Chile, for example, there is an area known as the Lake District, a charming Swiss-like region of snow-capped peaks, azure-blue lakes, and neat, old farmsteads. The main Andes are quite low here, with the peaks barely topping the 10,000-foot mark. Most are volcanoes—some, like Lonquimay, are active, and one of them, Osorno, is a perfectly shaped conical peak: the Fujiyama of Chile. The region is popular with climbers from Chile, but also quite a few Argentines come across the border to climb. Most of the peaks here have small huts called *refugios*, not dissimilar to those found in Europe, though in general they are not as well kept

Left: Paine Pass and Grey Glacier, Paine National Park, Patagonia, Chile

Above: Paine Grande

Below: Cordillera Paine

Overleaf: Approaching the summit of Volcán Osorno, Chile

or picturesque. The local climbing clubs that maintain and guard these huts usually do not have the financial resources of their European counterparts, but despite this, the huts are serviceable and handy.

My friend Gordon and I decided to go have a look at Osorno on our way to the Antarctic in 1986. Arriving at Puerto Montt by air from Santiago, we rented a car at the airport and reached the hut on Osorno by way of Lago Llanquihue, one of the classic lakes of the region. Osorno rose behind the lake in majestic sweeps, reflecting its icy cone in the lake's blue waters. In the small resort town of Puerto Varas, we made local inquiries as to a possible route on the peak, but were strongly dissuaded by several villagers from climbing the "killer mountain." We learned that in the previous year eight climbers had died from falls in crevasses and

Grey Lake,
Paine National
Park, Chile

Iceberg in
Gerlache Strait,
Antarctic
Peninsula

Antarctic
Peninsula,
near Esperanza
Base

from sudden storms, and that two helicopter pilots sent to rescue the injured had crashed their craft on the peak and had also perished. We were advised that a mishap was certain to befall us as well. While even from a long distance it was obvious that Osorno was very heavily glaciated and crevassed, we were told that its proximity to the South Pacific causes sudden, moist storms to engulf the peak without warning. With some trepidation we drove up the west slope of Osorno and checked into a small ski chalet of the local club. The fine weather had by now turned to fog, and before dusk it started to snow. By morning, high winds and poor visibility made an ascent impossible. We decided to wait it out for a day and visited the local tourist spot—the famous Petrohue waterfalls. We tried our hand at some fly fishing at Lago Todos los Santos, which is considered to be the finest trout-fishing lake around. Then we camped that night by Lago Llanquihue. The 5:00 A.M. sunrise the following morning woke me to a clear, bright day. Gordon and I simultaneously jumped out of our sleeping bags, ran for the car, drove off for the ski hut, and in less than an hour were on our way up the

Summit pitch on Volcán Osorno, Chile

mountain. As it was a clear and windless sunny day, we made excellent progress on the firm and steepening snow slopes, jumping crevasses here and there, with Gordon leading the way. Around 10:00 A.M. we reached the halfway mark, when, suddenly, a menacing large bank of thick cloud rolled our way from the west. We had been concentrating so hard on the climb that we had not noticed the storm until it was just about on us. Looking up at the summit, we could see high-velocity lenticular clouds curving over the top at an alarming speed. After a brief pow-wow, we decided to go for it and pressed on with renewed speed to reach the foot of the final summit mushroom, where a 30-foot vertical wall of ice confronted us. We were by now being shelled by ice particles, sleeting snow, rain, and a vicious wind. Visibility was reduced to perhaps an arm's length. Miraculously, Gordon found a narrow ice gully that cut into the wall, and minutes later he was on top, belaying me from above. Now on the summit, we were exposed to the full blast of the gale and unable to discern where exactly the very highest ground was, so each in turn ran out a full length of rope while the other remained in an anchored position by the gully—the critical point of the matter being not to miss our route for

the descent. After a quick yodel and a victory jump, we descended the gully, inching our way down the tricky crevassed slopes, our crampon marks of the ascent now having all but disappeared. After two hours of feeling our way down, we finally emerged below the storm front and walked off, drenched head to toe—but we were victorious.

Anyone who wishes to climb in this region, the northernmost fringe of Patagonia, must come well prepared to cope with these kinds of gales, which occur all along the southern tip of South America. As a rule, the farther south, the worse the weather. The region of Fitzroy is notorious for very bad storms, and the Paine Mountains have their share as well. But regardless of the climate, this is one of the most invigorating and wild regions left in the world—sparsely populated, abounding in wildlife, and having in addition an enormous ice cap that will test the skill and endurance of climbing generations yet unborn.

Huascarán

Cordillera Blanca, Andes, Peru

Huascarán is the highest mountain in Peru, a huge ice-covered mass looming from afar as one approaches by road from Huaraz, the main village of the Santa Valley. Once believed to be the highest peak in South America, Huascarán is the fourth-highest after Aconcagua (22,831′), Ojos del Salado (Inca for "the eyes of the desert"—22,572′), and Mercedario (22,211′), all of which are located further south on the Andean chain. near the Chile/Argentina crest.

Huascarán south summit (left) and north peak

The peak has two distinct summits; the higher South Summit (22,205′) and the North Peak (21,833′), first climbed in 1908 by Annie Peck, an American journalist. Traveling by sea and then across Peru on horseback with the Swiss Taugwalder guides, she became not only the first person to climb Huascarán but also the first woman to accomplish the highest climb of any peak in South America (and at the age of 61 at that!). In 1932 the German Alpine Club sent a large mountaineering and scientific expedition to the Cordillera Blanca, the Andean subrange where Huascarán reigns supreme. Four members of this team, among them the famous Austrian cartographer Erwin Schneider, made it to the South Summit.

The Cordillera Blanca is without doubt the most spectacular range of the entire Andes mountain chain that stretches 5,000 miles along the western edge of the South American continent, from northern Colombia to the southern tip of Chile. The Cordillera Blanca is well known to climbers and trekkers, as the range is unequaled in the world for serious mountaineering (other than the Himalaya). It is a tropical, high-altitude paradise where one can walk around in shorts at 14,000 feet amid lush vegetation and emerald lakes, below some of the most spectacular ice flutings, sharp mushroomed ridges, and plastered crests of snow—with nearly always a deep blue sky for backdrop.

Yanganuco Valley,
Cordillera Bianca

Huascarán is regularly visited by mountaineers from around the world, and despite its height and size it is not difficult for an experienced alpinist. Ice conditions are the main obstacle and change from year to year owing to the constant movement of the glaciers (Huascarán has the largest glaciers in the world's equatorial zone), but once the saddle (called Garganta) between the two peaks is reached, no further difficulties mar the climb to the top. The standard route begins at the western base camp (15,100′), which can be reached from the hamlet of Musho.

Easy access to this mountain and the other peaks in the range (more than 70 peaks rise over 18,000 feet) accounts for much of their popularity with tourists. Traveling a good motorable road in the Santa Valley, one can turn off onto side roads at a number of villages, such as Carhuaz (access for the Copa group of peaks), Mancos (for Huascarán), Yungay (for Huandoy), and Caras (for Santa Cruz and Alpamayo mountains). The Cordillera Blanca also features a large number of deep U-shaped valleys,

Santa Valley, Cordillera Blanca

Andean Condor

called *quebradas* that intersect the range. These afford additional access, if not by car then certainly by mule, donkey, or on foot.

In 1975 Huascarán was designated a national park by the Peruvian government. All land above 4,000 meters (about 13,000′) of the entire region (not just the area around Huascarán itself) was declared "Parque Nacional Huascarán," following efforts by dedicated mountaineers and enlightened politicians in Lima.

For a fine close-up look at the park and Huascarán, drive to Yungay, a town buried in its entirety during the devastating earthquake of 1970 (it has since been rebuilt). Turn off and drive east into the Quebrada Llanganuco, where the jade-green lakes of the same name reflect the glaciers of the peaks nearby. Continue along the steep hairpin turns to Llanganuco Pass (15,584′), the only passage road across the Cordillera. The views here are dramatic and unexcelled. Above looms the twin-summited Huascarán, while across the valley rise the famous Huandoy peaks (20,981′ and 20,853′), Pisco (a favorite acclimatization and trekking peak at 19,029′), the infamous Chacraraju (20,052′), long believed to be unclimbable because of its near-vertical ice flutings, and Chopicalqui (20,846′), another peak of breathtaking design. As foot trails also lead to the pass, one can elect to walk. Some of these trails predate the Incas, and the passes—sharp ridges of rock—were often enlarged by them to allow their livestock to cross the mountains.

Huaraz, the jumping-off point for a trip into the Cordillera Blanca, is well supplied with small hotels and offers guide services for climbing and trekking. Supplies for any journey into the mountains can easily be purchased here, and qualified guides are eager to take newcomers into their beloved "sierra."

Yerupajá

Cordillera Huayhuash, Andes, Peru

As mentioned in the previous chapter, in the Cordillera Blanca (the area containing Huascarán), one can quickly and easily approach the mountain of one's choice by driving along the Santa Valley highway to the nearest roadhead village. A rough track or a trail then leads to the base of the peak or into one of the many *quebradas*, from where a mountain is reached or a trek is started. This is not the case, however, in the Cordillera Huayhuash. Even though the Huayhuash range lies only 35 miles south of its big brother, the Blanca, the layout of the mountainscape is different. There are no transverse *quebradas* here that enable the trekker or climber to cross from east to west. One walks into or around the range. In addition, the Huayhuash is further inland (with only the summits of the highest peaks above intermediate ridges visible from the highway), thus requiring a two-day approach march.

In terms of scenic grandeur in Peru, the Cordillera Huayhuash is second only to the Blanca. Such a concentrated cluster of glaciated spires and sharp granitic peaks as are found in the Huayhuash simply does not exist anywhere else in the Andes. Since the entire massif is only 20 miles long and 15 miles wide, it is an ideal range around which to walk. This can be accomplished in 8 to 12 days, depending on interest and side trips.

The highest peak of this range is Yerupajá (21,768′), a towering, jagged peak flanked by smaller—but equally rugged—Yerupajá Chico (20,082′) and Siulá (20,814′). Three other summits rise above 20,000 feet, while another 20 or so top the 18,000-foot mark.

Yerupajá

Yerupajá, the second highest peak in Peru, was first climbed in 1950 by two Americans, Dave Harrah and Jim Maxwell. Prior to their visit, only one party of mountaineers visited the range, in 1936, at which time Erwin Schneider (cartographer of Huascarán) made the first ascent of Siulá. Yerupajá has been climbed by several routes since its first ascent, noteworthy of which is the west face by Leif Patterson and Jorge Peterek in 1966.

Patterson, who was most impressed with the difficulties of climbing in the Huayhuash, called the northeast face "perhaps the finest challenge in all Peru." That face, also known as the Amazon face of Yerupajá, was climbed by Chris Jones and Paul Dix in 1968. Finally, the 5,000-foot south face fell in 1977 to Britons Rab Carrington and Alan Rouse.

None of the peaks here are easy. One of the most difficult climbs yet accomplished is the obelisk of Jirishanca, a nearly 20,000-foot spire, which has also been called the Matterhorn of Peru. A close neighbor of Yerupajá, Jirishanca has attracted attention from the world's best climbers.

For those who prefer to look around and contemplate mountains rather than climb them, the circuit around the Huayhuash is definitely one of the most spectacular treks in South America. Starting from the small roadside village of Chiquián, the traveler takes a two-to-three-day journey to reach the big peaks. The trip is never devoid of breathtaking scenery as the snow-capped ridges and hidden lakes of this exquisite mountain paradise unfold. During the first portion of the trek, the highlight

On trek in the Cordillera Huayhuash

is beautiful Laguna Jahuacocha and its twin, Soltera Cocha, both of which lie at the foot of Jirishanca at 13,000 feet. The second part of the trek takes one over the Continental Divide (Punta Cacanam) and into the eastern flank of the range. Here, a small lake, Laguna Ninacocha, is believed to be the source of the Amazon. Further south lies Laguna Carhuacocha, which mirrors the great Amazon face of Yerupajá in its

Yerupajá, Yerupajá Chico, and Jirishanca Chico in the Cordillera Huayhuash

dark-blue waters. After crossing an easy pass (Portachuelo), one reaches the southern end of the range. Then it is time to head north again. Crossing back, west via the Punta Cuyoc, the final stage of the circuit now presents itself. One can either descend to Huayllapa and continue north to Chiquián or descend to Cajatambo, where transportation is available to the lowlands and back to Lima.

Aconcagua

Central Andes, Argentina

In 1897 the Swiss mountain guide Matthias Zurbriggen became the first known person to stand on the highest point in the Western Hemisphere, an ancient and enormous volcano 22,831 feet high in the central Andes of Argentina. Yet he may not have been the first human to reach the highest mountain outside Asia, as remnants of what appear to be Inca stone walls have since been found as high as 21,000 feet on the peak. If the Incas were capable of building such structures at these elevations—presumably enclosures to keep llamas for sacrificial purposes—then it must also be assumed that they were able to reach the summit, since their religious worship traditionally took place on mountain summits.

Aconcagua is high indeed, but it is not a mountain of great alpine beauty. The peak, a disintegrating hulk of metamorphic rock, is extremely old geologically. Evidence of age is present everywhere—in the dark yellow convoluted rockbands that surround the mountain and in the ochre, brown, and reddish colors of ancient molten fumaroles, eroded lava tubes, and endless scree slopes. The few glaciers are bare and wilted into terminals of fantastically shaped ice pinnacles, some up to 50 feet tall. Exceptions are the Polish Glacier and the icefalls on the south face, both spectacular glaciers. The area around Aconcagua is equally desolate: the land is uninhabited, arid, and empty. The valleys that lead to the mountain from Puente del Inca (a stop on the Trans-Andean railroad that links Santiago, Chile, to Mendoza, Argentina) are long, hot, and dry. Yet there is a special mood, a unique atmosphere that lingers in the air near this king of the Andes, a feeling of timelessness, of endless space.

Aconcagua

The first Western man to attempt the "Stone Sentinel" (as the Indian word for Aconcagua translates) was Paul Gussfeldt, a German doctor. He reached 21,600 feet in 1883 after his Chilean companions had collapsed from exhaustion and frostbite. He tried again ten days later but was repelled by a snowstorm. Then, in 1897, the English mountaineer and explorer Edward FitzGerald arrived at the scene, accompanied by Zurbriggen and four Swiss porters. After a long, laborious struggle along the now-standard route, Zurbriggen reached the summit alone; FitzGerald stopped 500 feet lower due to the altitude and exhaustion.

Other routes have since been pioneered on Aconcagua; the most popular among mountaineers now is the "Polish" route, a line on the northeast side of the peak, first climbed by a Polish team in 1934 under the leadership of Victor Ostrowski. This route offers a fairly good challenge along the Polish Glacier and is generally preferred over the uninteresting bare scree and pumice slopes of the normal route on the north face. The most outstanding technically difficult route—the 10,000-foot south face—was pioneered by the French in 1954 under René Ferlet and Lucien Berardini. The team set out to attack this formidable precipice in alpine style and reached the summit after nine days of continuous climbing and bivouacking. Frostbitten and exhausted, they descended the normal route and were found later that night by a Chilean rescue party that had set out from the base camp hut to search for them. It was, at that time, the hardest climb ever accomplished in South America, on one of the world's greatest precipices.

Located entirely in Argentina, Aconcagua is usually approached from

West face of Tupungato

Mendoza, Argentina's wine-producing capital at the edge of the vast interior *pampa*. Interesting colonial architecture, festivals, vintage wines, and sidewalk cafes provide entertainment for the mountaineer, who sometimes must wait days before the authorities complete the paperwork required for a permit to climb the mountain. Once all documents are in order, climbers proceed by train, bus, or car to Puente del Inca, the starting point of the trek to base camp. The track to the normal route follows the arid and hot Horcones Valley through sparsely vegetated canyons, where, aside from a tiny edible berry called the *calafate* and some spiny ground cover, little grows. This is the eastern flank of the Andes, in the shadow of the Pacific storms and gales that blow in from Chile. There is some wildlife: llamalike guanacos, Patagonia hares, occasional

armadillos, and Andean condors, stately flyers, with a wingspan up to 15 feet. Base camp is at Plaza de Mulas (14,400′). From this point on there is a small foot trail that leads to Camp I, Refugio Antartida (18,300′), and Camp II, Refugio Plantamura (20,050′). From the latter a faint track continues to above a large scree slope, called Gran Accareo, from where a steep gully, La Canaleta (studded with large, unstable boulders) leads to the crest.

Then, after traveling nearly half a mile above 22,000 feet, one can finally stand on Aconcagua's pinnacle, staring off into the distant void. Nothing obstructs the view, as this is the highest point on the South American continent, as well as in the entire Western Hemisphere—there isn't anything higher for 10,000 miles around!

Licancábur

Northern Andes, Chile

The Spanish conquest of Chile, which occurred in the 16th century shortly after the fall of the Inca Empire, was largely organized from the Inca capital in Peru, Cuzco, by one of Spain's lesser-known conquistadores, Pedro de Valdivia. Valdivia began his conquest of Chile in 1540 with an army of 200 cuirassed Spanish soldiers and approximately 2,000 Peruvian Indians for support. He traversed the entire length of Chile, crossing the fearsome Atacama Desert, to what is today the city of Santiago, which he founded in 1541. During his passage of the Atacama, he founded the town of San Pedro de Atacama alongside a large oasis at the foot of a shapely, triangular peak—Licancábur (19,455′), an extinct volcano crowned with a circular rim and a small lake, the highest in the world.

The Atacama Desert consists of a large interior valley, bordered to the west by the Barros Arana foothills and to the east by the *puna* and the enormous northern Andes of Chile. The desert itself reaches well beyond territorial boundaries and extends into Bolivia and Peru. Here one finds the largest salt pans in South America, known locally as *salars*. The largest of these is the Salar de Uyuni in Bolivia, just across the border from Chile. Also in the Atacama Desert is the Salar de Atacama, a wide shimmering expanse of salt crystals 60 miles long by 40 miles wide.

At the time of Valdivia's establishment of San Pedro, the Atacama Desert was inhabited by local tribes known as Atacameños, whose ancestry dates back to 1000–1500 B.C. These Indians lived peacefully under Inca overlords in the shadow of Licancábur, cultivating crops in the fertile oasis. Nearby a large fortress had been built along the backbone of a rocky promontory, known today as the *Pukara* (fortress) of Quitor. Here the natural escarpment protected them from unknown (but always potential) assailants. Surrounding the central desert were the Andes Mountains, which were sacred to the Atacameños as well as to the Incas. The snows that collected on their summits between June and August provided abundant water for the oases, which spread here and there among the vast desert landscapes between the foothills to the west and the high *puna* (highlands) of the Andes. The peaks, among them such giants as Llullaillaco (22,057′), Ojos del Salado (22,589′), and Incahuasi (21,657′), were easy scrambles for the Indians, and on the summits they worshipped their sun gods. So it is that Licancábur has a pile of wood on the crater rim left by these early inhabitants of more than 500 years ago. According to archaeologist Charles Brush, who climbed Licancábur in 1983 and used scuba gear to explore the lake's murky bottom, the wood was brought to the summit for signaling, for making offerings to the gods, and also for keeping warm while sacrificial ceremonies took place. Eight ruins (possibly shelters) also remain on the summit.

Licancábur

Although San Pedro de Atacama is now a peaceful and tranquil oasis, Licancábur was witness to one of the most savage battles in Chile's conquest, the Spanish taking of Quitor. The heavily fortified *Pukara* was attacked by Don Francisco de Aguirre (a lieutenant under Valdivia), who was accompanied by 30 mounted Spaniards armed with *arquebuses*, or muskets. More than 1,000 Indians, who had seen neither horse nor gun, died within one and a half hours; the heads of the leaders were cut off by the bloodthirsty conquistadores and exposed on the ramparts of the fort.

Today, San Pedro de Atacama (8,000′) is a thriving, if small, oasis in the center of a vast desert, far removed from the modern world. The area is rich in archaeological finds and boasts a superb museum, founded by the Belgian Father Le Paige (1904–1980), where 15,000 years of human evolution may be traced. The museum contains over 300,000 archaeological specimens—many collected by Father Le Paige—including several mummies, one of these being the famous ancient remains of a young girl called "Miss Chile." The Church of San Pedro was built by Valdivia in 1540 and reconstructed in 1730, using local materials such as cactus wood, reeds (for thatching), clay, and straps of llama leather (replacing nails). In the plaza, across from this pleasant colonial church and surrounded by ancient large pepper trees, is the historical house of Valdivia, built for him by de Aguirre in 1540. It is from this modest house that the final conquest of Chile was planned.

For the visitor to these high, desert mountains, the problems are mainly access, altitude, and water. While public transportation is available to San Pedro, it is difficult to get close to the mountains. Occasionally a mining truck will come by, but it is preferable to have a vehicle of one's own. The Indian trail that leads to the summit of Licancábur starts from a base camp on the eastern saddle (15,000′) at the Chile/Bolivia border. It is necessary to cross into Bolivia for a very short distance to reach this saddle, which can be approached by a four-wheel-drive vehicle. From this area a path leads to the summit. Most parties make a high camp at approximately 17,000 feet and hike to the summit the next day. For the very hardy there is a record-setting high-altitude swim in the icy waters of the crater lake!

Valley of the Moon in the Atacama Desert

El Tatio thermal geysers on altiplano

Licancábur and wild llamas on altiplano

Cactus of the Coastal Desert

Volcán Osorno

Northern Patagonian Andes, Chile

The Northern Patagonian Andes, rich in forests, sky-blue lakes, and green meadows, are topped with glaciated volcanoes and sharp, ice-clad granite peaks. The area, which lies between latitudes 38° and 42° south, has often been referred to as the "Switzerland of South America" and somewhat resembles the Pacific Northwest, although the highest peak, Cerro Lanín, is only 12,195 feet. The central part of this region, known as the Chilean and Argentine Lake District, is the most visited and indeed the more accessible part of these mountains, as the average elevation of the crest rarely exceeds 3,000 feet. There are, however, some fine peaks here, enough to justify a long flight from the United States for a climbing holiday.

The most visible—and therefore the most famous—mountains on the Chilean side are the volcanoes Lonquimay (9,481′), from whose crater billow clouds of hot steam, Llaima (10,252′), Lanín, and Osorno (8,727′), a dormant volcano entirely clad in a thick glacial mantle. On the Argentine side, the peaks receive less precipitation and thus are more suited to rock climbing. The highest peak and perhaps most often climbed is Cerro Tronador (11,386′), a rock-and-ice peak on the border with access mainly from the Argentine side. Further east and centered around San Carlos de Bariloche, a popular resort town for the Buenos Aires crowds who flock there both in summer and in winter, are a number of fine rock peaks, such as Torre Catedral, Tres Picos, and Lopez.

Volcán Osorno

Known as the Fujiyama of the Lake District, Volcán Osorno was first climbed in 1948 by Jan Renous, who also made the first ascent of Calbuco, a smaller peak to the south. The standard route is from theTeski Ski Club hut, on the west side just below the ski lift. A dirt road leads to this hut, which is fully equipped with a dormitory, washrooms, and a restaurant. CONAF (the Chilean equivalent of the National Park Service) has an office here, where climbers wishing to attempt Osorno must register. The mountain is famous for tempestuous weather due to its proximity to the sea and is regarded by the local inhabitants as a killer mountain. The only difficulty of the standard or west-face route, which is moderately crevassed, is the ice wall just below the summit. There are other routes on this beautiful but dangerous mountain; however, none are recommended. A great many accidents have occurred on the peak, mainly because of its seemingly easy slopes and low angle. Nevertheless, the weather and the treacherous crevasses one encounters everywhere make it a peak that should not be underestimated. In 1976 the well-known German alpinist Gunther Hauser died on Osorno; apparently while on a solo climb, he fell in a crevasse and was unable to extricate himself.

Access to the Lake District is not complicated. There is air service from Santiago to Puerto Montt, the jumping-off point for the Chilean peaks, and from Buenos Aires to San Carlos, for those who prefer to start from the Argentine side. There is, however, a great deal of tourist traffic. From Puerto Montt, proceed by bus or car to Puerto Varas, a pleasant and relaxed holiday resort on large Lago Llanquihue, across from Osorno. From the shore of the lake the view of Osorno is unsurpassed, and few mountaineers are able to resist the temptation to reach for the snowline, strap on a pair of crampons, and head for the summit. A road leads along the south shore to the

Opposite:
The upper slopes
of Volcán Osorno

Lago Llanquihue,
below Volcán Osorno

village of Ensenada, and from there it is just a short drive to the 5,000-foot level and the Teski hut, from where the climbing begins. To continue to Argentina, drive from Ensenada to Petrohue and take the ferry across Lago Todos Los Santos to Peulla and Puerto Blest—which leads via a series of ferries and short bus rides, all interconnecting with one another, to Bariloche.

The Lake District of Chile and Argentina comes highly recommended. The area is well laid out and has good huts and trails. The climbing is relaxed and straightforward, the food is outstanding, and, best of all, there are very few people around.

Paine Grande

Cordillera Paine, Chile

Near the southern tip of South America, where the Andes' 5,000-mile-long chain of mountains comes to an abrupt end and plunges into the stormy South Pacific, surges the Paine Range—a spectacular array of huge spires and sharp peaks with gleaming, smooth walls rising for 6,000 vertical feet out of the undulating Patagonian grasslands.

This is a wild land of wind-whipped lakes, billowing skies, and rolling hills, with the bleak aspect of Yorkshire moors on a stormy day in midwinter. It is also a land of endless *pampa*, home to millions of sheep and cattle, tended by tall and rugged mustachioed men, the *gauchos* and the *huasos*, famed cowboys of the South American prairie.

The Paine mountains, which enchant trekker, climber, and tourist alike with their incomparable, stark beauty, are a distinct range of peaks connected to the main Andean chain by a mountain pass, the Paso Paine. The range runs in a west-east direction, as opposed to the Andes' north-south axis. The length, slightly less than 30 miles, makes it a compact and easily accessible range.

The Torres del Paine, as the area is known in Chile, is an upthrusted batholith—a gigantic bubble of once-molten granite—that rose from the center of the earth long ago and later was covered with large glaciers that came streaming off the continental icecap during the Ice Age. In time, the glaciers retreated, carving huge towers and deep gashes into the "bubble." What remains today are the alpine peaks and wondrous Towers of Paine.

Paine Grande

One would be hard-pressed to find anywhere in the world a more compelling, savagely beautiful array of peaks than the Towers of Paine. The steepness and size of the smooth granite walls defy the imagination. The mountains are surrounded by strings of many large and small lakes of different color and shape, varying from bright blue to turquoise green to pale gray. The hills and valleys that surround the peaks are heavily forested and support a wealth of indigenous flora, including wind-twisted beech trees (both Magellan and Haya, or Southern beech).

The wildlife at Paine is abundant, with over 4,000 guanacos (cousins of the llama) roaming the park. Armadillo, puma, fox, Patagonia hare, and rhea (the Patagonian version of the ostrich) can also be seen. But most bountiful are the avian species, of which upland geese, parrots, flamingos, and Andean condors are the most visible. Here one can see the regal condor, the world's largest flying bird, effortlessly riding the wind currents around the peaks and towers on its 12-foot wingspan.

Rock climbers and mountaineers from around the world come to the Paine massif to test their mettle against the formidable rock walls that only recently have fallen to the persistent sieges laid on them. Some alpinists visited this area in the late 1800s, but the first peaks, small ones, were not climbed until the mid-1930s. The area became known internationally to climbers in the late 1950s with the first ascent of Paine Grande (10,600′), the highest peak, by an Italian party led by Guido Monzino. This difficult peak dominates the mountain range from the west and is encrusted year-round with a thick upper layer of cakey ice.

The Paine mountain chain is shaped in a rough figure "8," with an entrance at both ends. One can thus visit its two "inner sanctuaries" for a spectacular close-up

view of the peaks. At the southern entrance stands the famous Cuerno, or horn, a stunning shark's fin of granite, topped off with dark-gray slate, a result of the geological uplift.

After the Paine Grande was climbed, the Towers and the Cuerno were the next to be scaled. The Italians were most active, but notable ascents have also been made by British, South African, and Spanish climbers. From the north entrance of the figure "8" it is possible to gain access to the famous spires, the South, Central, and North Towers, respectively 8,200, 8,070, and 7,380 feet. The Central Tower has the biggest vertical face of rock, its east face measuring over 4,000 feet from the glacier to the top.

Today the Paine massif is the centerpiece of the Torres del Paine National Park, crown jewel among Chile's parks, established by the government in 1959. In 1979 UNESCO declared it "a reserve of the biosphere" because of its unique mountain scenery and its unaltered state.

Although the Paine Mountains are far from the United States—about as far as one can travel south—they are nevertheless relatively easy to approach after the long journey by air to Punta Arenas (a boom town thriving on the recent oil exploration in the Strait of Magellan). From Punta, as it is affectionately called by hikers and climbers alike, daily bus service is available to Puerto Natales, a small, near-forgotten fishing village on the shores of Ultima Esperanza Sound. From here tourist buses now visit the park in the summer, although no regular bus service exists. Taxis are also available for the three-and-a-half-hour journey.

Several campsites are located near the park headquarters as well as a local inn, Posada Serrano, and a hotel. A small store has most of the food items a trekker might want. From this base it is possible to undertake interesting hikes to see the peaks up close, though, if the weather cooperates, the most spectacular panoramas of the southern escarpment are to be had from the central area near the hotel.

For those who wish to hike, two three-day trips are worth considering. Both provide access to the figure "8." The first allows one to see the Cuernos from the southern sanctuary and many other stunning spires, such as the Espada and a close-up view of Paine Grande. The second hike takes one around to the north side of the area to view the Towers. For this trip it is best to rent a car or taxi to the Paine River, then hike up the Ascensio River to the lake at the base of the three towers. Well-equipped travelers who have more time may consider one of the finest walking trips anywhere: the 6- or 7-day hike around the entire Paine Range.

The weather is generally favorable in November and in March, although December and February can also be good. Avoid January as this is the rainy season, and also a time when many South Americans are on holiday.

Left: Climbing near Paine Pass

Overleaf: Grey River in the Cordillera Paine

Left: Icebergs of the Antarctic Peninsula

Right: The Adelie Penguin Colony, below Mt. Taylor

Mt. Taylor

Antarctic Peninsula, Antarctica

The Antarctic Peninsula is an 800-mile-long curving tentacle of rock and ice that sweeps off the continent of Antarctica. Pointing north toward South America, it is separated from the Western Hemisphere by the Scotia Sea and the infamous Drake Passage, a rip-roaring 600-mile-wide channel of tempestuous water connecting the South Atlantic Ocean with the South Pacific Ocean.

The peninsula can be divided into three major geographical regions: Palmer Land, Graham Land, and the Trinity Peninsula at the very tip. Here the land tapers to a long and narrow spine with mountains rising to 3,000 feet. The last peaks of any size at land's end are Mt. Taylor (3,274′) and Mt. Bransfield (2,490′), the two mountains in Antarctica furthest from the South Pole. In the shadow of these ice-clad peaks lies Hope Bay, the first harbor of the peninsula (known to the Argentines and Chileans as Bahia Esperanza), and historic Hut Cove. South of the Trinity Peninsula lies Graham Land, where the landmass doubles in width and the peaks rise to 6,000 feet. Graham Land extends for 350 miles, half the length of the entire peninsula. Connecting this long arc of rock and ice to the Antarctic mainland is Palmer Land, by far the largest and highest region, with peaks up to 11,000 feet, including Mt. Jackson (11,319′), which remains unclimbed.

Located at approximately 63° 15′ S, Hope Bay (or Esperanza) is the site of a large Argentine base. Previously this was the location of the British base at Hut Cove, but it was closed and now only the Argentines remain active at Esperanza, where they have established their principal presence on the continent. About 75 people inhabit the base, including children who were born there and a small army detachment.

The discovery of Antarctica dates back to 1820. It was in that year that the continent was first sighted and claimed by British, American, and Russian navigators. Credit for the initial view of the "last continent" is now generally given to the Russian navigator Admiral von Bellingshausen, who sighted land to the far north of the continent. Edward Bransfield, an English sea captain, was the first to sight the peninsula, on January 30, 1820, three days after Bellingshausen's claim. American historians

Left: Above Esperanza on Mt. Flora

Right: An iceberg in Drake Passage

prefer to believe Nathaniel Palmer, a 19-year-old sealer from New England, sighted the mainland in November 1820, which he described as "sterile and dismal." None of these early navigators were able to land, however, and it took a year before John Davis, another American sealer, became the first man to set foot on the Antarctic continent. Davis landed at Hughes Bay in Graham Land, halfway down the Gerlache Strait that separates Anvers Island—with the highest peak north of 65° S, Mt. Francais (9,455′)—from the mainland.

Although Mt. Taylor could perhaps be climbed in one long day from Hut Cove—the total travel distance to the mountain is not more than 10 miles—the terrain is continuously glaciated and heavily crevassed, and the weather at the tip of the peninsula is extremely unreliable. The obvious route is via Nobby Nunatak and Summit Pass (1,138′)—Argentine maps show this as "Paso del Medio"—around Thimble Peak and across the Mondor Glacier to the base of the southwest ridge and then to the summit. This climb should not be attempted without first securing permission from the Argentine base, and it should be undertaken only by experienced and well-equipped mountaineers who are fully aware of the tempestuous storms or katabatic winds that can descend without warning on these parts of the peninsula.

Wildlife on the peninsula and on the outlying islands, as well as on the South Shetlands across the Bransfield Strait, is abundant and varied. A colony of penguins resides at Hope Bay, which is perhaps one of the biggest concentrations of Adelies on the Antarctic. Gentoo and chinstrap penguins also visit, though the only species that nest on the continent are the Adelie and the Emperor, the largest. Weddell seals (named after James Weddell, a British sea captain who in 1823 sailed south further than any man before him—reaching 74° 14′—into the sea that also bears his name), crabeater seals, and the predatory leopard seals sun themselves on the sandy beaches and large ice floes. Humpback whales cavort along the coast with other species such as the sperm, minke, and killer whales. All of this activity can readily be seen from any cruise ship or vessel underway.

However exciting the penguins, seals, and whales may be, the truly unique spectacle is the countless millions of birds that inhabit the peninsula, both shoreline birds that live and catch their food along the coast and the even more numerous pelagic birds that inhabit the open ocean. The most commonly known species are cormorants, terns, Antarctic skuas, sheathbills, and petrels, including the wandering albatross, of which 24 different species breed south of the Antarctic Convergence.

EUROPE

Europe, especially Western Europe, is the birthplace of mountain climbing—or alpinism—where it has been a popular sport, if not an institution, for over a century. Those countries that share the Alps—France, Italy, Germany, Switzerland, and Austria—have large alpine clubs with hundreds of thousands of members, extensive networks of mountain huts, and big budgets. It's all part of the hotel and tourism industry, which caters to millions of Europeans who climb, hike, backpack, and ski in the mountains. As a result, the Alps are somewhat overdeveloped with roads, viaducts, dams, cable cars, and hotels—and with people crowding the shrinking open spaces. This is especially noticeable in the more popular alpine regions such as central Switzerland. Telepherique cables are strung everywhere (now even to the top of the Kleine Matterhorn), and cog railroads lead to high mountain saddles, where large restaurants cater to 2,000 tourists a day who come up for lunch

The Hörnli Ridge of the Matterhorn, Italian /Swiss Alps

Aosta, Italy

and a quick view. Even in the rustic old villages one finds tall hotels, and even higher condominiums. It therefore comes as no surprise to surmise that mountain climbing in the Alps is different from anywhere else in the world. It is an institutionalized sport with strict rules, national climbing schools, formal programs, and licensed mountain guides. It is nearly impossible to climb the Matterhorn by yourself nowadays without being hassled by the local guide bureau who wants its share of the action. On a typical, clear, summer climbing day in Chamonix, France, one of the most popular climbing centers in the Alps (if not the world), the local aerial tram to the Aiguille du Midi—a vertical lift of nearly 8,000 feet—will have a waiting crowd of climbers ready to jam into the 6:00 A.M. car, not dissimilar to the busy weekend ski resort activity in Squaw Valley or Aspen. Only here the crowd consists of climbers loaded with packs, ropes, crampons, and ice axes. Off they rush from the top of the tram to the base of their chosen mountain, and often those not quick enough must wait their turn to climb.

Col du Géant,
Mont Blanc Range,
France/Italy

Last summer I returned to the Alps with my wife, Nadia, for a visit as a photographer, not a climber, drove to Breuil-Cervinia (the southern and less crowded approach to the Matterhorn), and spent the night in a mountain hut near the Matterhorn in order to take pictures at dawn. We had come up by aerial tramway from Breuil to the Theodule Col, the 11,000-foot pass on the south side of the Matterhorn, where a fine old hut is situated. While we were busy devouring our evening meal of minestrone, pasta, and cheese, we talked with the guardian of the hut. "The Matterhorn," he complained, "has not been climbed as yet this season [it's August 8]. The weather has been bad, with lots of snow and continuous overcasts. It's the worst summer in 30 years and business is bad." Out of the corner of a window the massive base of the great mountain rose dramatically from the land below. The summit was heavily cloaked in thick, swirling clouds and the weather forecast for the next day was not good. It did not affect us, however, as we did not come to climb, but to reminisce and to enjoy, for this is one of the spots in the world that I cherish, a place drenched in alpine history. Here, in this hut, we were but a stone's throw from the most famous and beautiful mountain in the world.

Dent du Géant
and Grandes
Jorasses,
Mont Blanc Range,
France/Italy

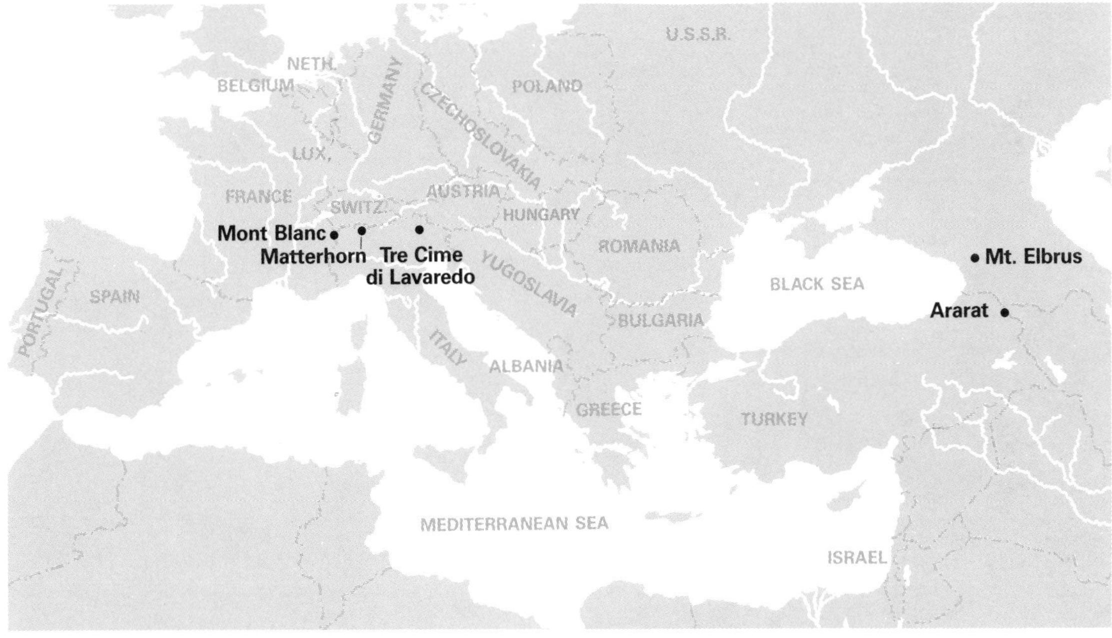
U.S.S.R.
NETH.
BELGIUM
GERMANY
POLAND
CZECHOSLOVAKIA
LUX.
FRANCE
SWITZ.
AUSTRIA
HUNGARY
Mont Blanc
Matterhorn
Tre Cime
di Lavaredo
ROMANIA
Mt. Elbrus
PORTUGAL
SPAIN
YUGOSLAVIA
BLACK SEA
BULGARIA
Ararat
ITALY
ALBANIA
GREECE
TURKEY
MEDITERRANEAN SEA
ISRAEL

To mountain historians, the sport of alpinism took a quantum leap here in 1865 with Edward Whymper's first ascent.

After dinner we crawled into our down sleeping bags (the rooms are not heated) in a private double-bunk room. I set the alarm for 4:00 A.M. hoping to photograph the sunrise on the Matterhorn. When the buzzer rang, I jumped out of my bag, looked out of the backdoor that was down the hall, and luck was with me! The entire eastern sky was ablaze and all the peaks were visible—the Gornergrat, the Zinal Rothhorn, the Alalin Horn, the Steck Horn, and, closer by, looming above, the Breithorn. To my left was the Matterhorn, still wrapped in darkness except for the very summit tip, which just at that moment caught a pale salmon tint. After shooting a couple of rolls of film, I finally rested and watched the soft pink light as it slowly sank down the east face and Whymper's famous Hornli ridge, which I had climbed several times over 20 years ago. Far below and to the north lay Zermatt, barely visible in the first light.

I originally came to the Alps in 1960, visiting Switzerland as a tourist. The mountains made a strong impression on me and awakened an urge to be among them. I visited again in the following years, meanwhile having migrated from my native country of Belgium to California. In 1963 I returned to explore and climb in the Dolomites as well as in the French Alps, and also to organize the first alpine outings for the Sierra Club in Europe. After that, visits to the Alps became an annual pilgrimage. In 1968 I visited the Matterhorn for the first time and climbed it with a group of friends. All I remember of that experience now is getting to the top of the narrow, snow-covered summit ridge and walking over to the Italian side, where stood a large, hand-wrought iron cross. It was a bright and clear day and the view from the summit remains unforgettable to this day.

The Matterhorn at sunrise, Italian/Swiss Alps

Finally, my wife and I departed, returning to Breuil. As we descended with the cable car, I craved for a last close-up look of that old friend the Matterhorn. And even though I have since traveled the world and seen the biggest peaks to be found, there is no mountain quite like the Matterhorn.

When viewing the European mountains, one must of course also include the Caucasus, a most formidable range in the European part of the Soviet Union. Mt. Elbrus (18,481′), the highest summit of the Caucasus, is also the highest peak in Europe. Before visiting the Matterhorn last year, Nadia and I made a trip to Russia and climbed this huge extinct volcano. We flew to Moscow, then on to Mineralye Vodne, and from there by bus to Azau (7,600′), the roadhead for climbing Elbrus. Here Sovalpsport, the official U.S.S.R. climbing organization, put us up at a large sports hotel from where we would start the climb.

The Russians were extremely courteous, going out of their way to make us feel at ease and to provide a mountain ambience. I was introduced to a crafty-looking older gentleman. Husein Zalihanov Chokkaevich was the Director of State, Master of Sports of the U.S.S.R., and Chairman of the Mountaineering Federation of the Kabardinian-Balkarian Autonomous Republic. He paced around the courtyard of our climbing lodge, at the foot of Mt. Elbrus, like a caged lion. With him was the local TV reporting crew and a crowd of Russian climbers and guides. He was wearing basketball shoes and a sweatsuit and, on his hip, a service revolver. He was keen to interview our American climbing party for the local TV station. "Are you here to help celebrate the 70th anniversary of the Russian Revolution?" he asked. "Why not, sounds good to me!" I replied. On the air, he asked and talked about Ronald Reagan, Gorbachev, *perestroika* (no comment). Then Soviet/American mountaineering . . .

Priutt Hut on Mt. Elbrus, Caucasus, Soviet Union

Ha! Here I had an answer: "The climbers from our country are continuing with meaningful exchange programs, who are hopefully contributing to the improvement of ties of culture and friendship between the two countries." The chairman beamed. He immediately invited me to climb Elbrus with his group—all 400 of them! It turned out that he was the head of a government-sponsored youth group who were to climb Elbrus in celebration of the Revolution. I knew that Elbrus was a popular mountain in the U.S.S.R., but 400 all at one time?

The following morning we were up and off early (no sign of the 400 climbers yet) and reached the big aluminum-sheeted Priutt Refuge on Elbrus by midafternoon—by a combination of cable car and chairlift, and a two-hour hike up the glacier. The hut resembled an oversized Airstream trailer, with room for about 60 climbers. The next day while we rested and acclimatized, the 400 Soviet climbers finally showed up. Fortunately, they camped on a level area about a quarter of a mile from the hut. The chairman, however, had his own private quarters in the refuge and came in style, riding a large snowcat. More interviews, more TV cameras. He has climbed Elbrus 34 times. In fact, he helped build a small hut on the saddle between the two summits (now in ruins). He also has an eight-year-old son by a fourth wife . . . what a guy! He motioned to me to join him in his private digs and offered me vodka, two handfuls of apples, and an invitation to a bear hunt! He then pulled out a bottle of champagne from his pack, which he quickly hid again. "For your victory," he said with a broad grin. Only after giving another speech, this time to his entire 400-man army, again extolling the virtues of friendship, cooperation, and *glasnost*, was I allowed to rejoin the company of my friends and to retire.

The next morning we were out of the hut by 4:00 A.M., headlamps casting tiny islands of light on a gigantic dormant volcano, crampons crunching the Styrofoam snow. As dawn struck, we were well on our way, reaching a small rock band known as the Pastukhov outcrop, around 16,000 feet. The feared 400 had left about two hours ahead of us, and their tracks had now become visible. As more light appeared, we could see the long line of tiny figures reaching the saddle between the two summits high above us. It was cold, but not as cold as I had expected. A friend, Bruce Klepinger, a mountaineer with more than 1,000 ascents to his name, had warned me that Elbrus was a very cold mountain, in fact, the coldest he had ever been on. The day was clear and windless, however, and by 8:00 A.M. we were in the sun. The climb of Elbrus is technically easy, requiring only an ice axe and crampons under good conditions. We reached the saddle and rested there while the Soviets descended from the summit. They were all over the place! Fortunately they were soon gone, and we could resume our ascent. The summit was reached at 11:00 A.M. The weather was clear and warm and allowed for stupendous views of the main Caucasus range and views into Georgia. I looked for Ararat, 100 miles to the south, but there was haze across the southern horizon. When we arrived back at the Priutt Refuge four hours later, our friend the chairman was waiting . . . champagne, vodka, speeches . . . and watermelon! Nothing ever tasted so good. "To the Revolution, to Elbrus, and to friendship!" Ahh, those Russians . . . they know how to live.

View from Mt. Elbrus of the Caucasus Range (Ushba to the left), Soviet Union

Mont Blanc

Alps, France/Italy

The reigning monarch of the Alps, Mont Blanc (15,771′), is the highest peak in Western Europe. Straddling the Italian-French frontier (the Italians call the mountain Monte Bianco), Mont Blanc is at once majestic, massive, and complex; a veritable mountain chain with no less than 30 major glaciers and surrounded by a score of steep rock peaks. On the north side of this impressive wall lies the French town of Chamonix, a world center for mountaineering, while on the southern, or Italian, side can be found the picturesque alpine villages of Courmayeur and Entrèves. These alpine towns are steeped in the lore of Mont Blanc and mountaineering history, for it is here that Alpinism was born some 200 years ago.

One of the first men to look at Mont Blanc with an eye to climbing it was Swiss scientist/naturalist Horace de Saussure (1740–1799), who, from his first visit to Chamonix at age 20, dreamed of making the ascent. After viewing Mont Blanc from Le Brévent, a high hill north of the Chamonix Valley, de Saussure was so enthralled with what he saw that, on returning to the village, he offered a monetary reward to the first man who could find a route to the top. He himself made several attempts and finally realized his dream in 1787, reaching the summit 27 years after his obsession began. Alas, he was not to be the first, although that does not seem to have bothered him.

The first ascent of the peak was recorded by a young Chamonix crystal hunter, Jacques Balmat, in 1786. Balmat was one of a party who set out to find the route in order to collect the prize money offered by de Saussure. When this group of guides reached a point on the mountain somewhere above the Dôme du Goûter, they could not proceed further and retreated to Chamonix. Balmat, however, thinking perhaps he had spotted a route, decided to remain behind without telling his companions of his observations. Soon the others were gone and Balmat was alone. He spent a cold and miserable night in a hole in the snow. When daylight came he started up and soon came to the conclusion that if he could cross a series of crevasses along the Grand Plateau, the route to the top would be free and clear. In his own words:

Mont Blanc from the Italian side

Overleaf: Aiguille Noire de Peuterey, Mont Blanc, and Brenva Glacier

> In descending [the previous day] to the Grand Plateau, I thought that halfway down there was a steep but possible slope, which would lead to the Rocher Rouge. I determined to try it, but when I reached it I found it was so steep and the snow so hard that I could not stand on it. However, by cutting steps with my baton I managed to climb it, but my fatigue was extreme. It was neither easy nor pleasant to hang, so to speak, on one leg with an abyss below me, and obliged to cut steps like a staircase. At length I reached the Rocher Rouge. "Oh!" I said, "we are nearly there. From here to the top of Mount Blanc there is nothing to stop me." But I was half dead with fatigue, cold, and hunger. It was getting late and I was obliged to descend, but with the determination of returning the first opportunity and I felt sure of success.

He returned to Chamonix totally exhausted and fell ill, no doubt because of his night out in the snow without protection. Attended to by the village physician, Dr.

Michel Paccard, he confided his secret and the details of his ascent and offered to take the good doctor along on his next attempt. Dr. Paccard agreed, and on August 8, 1786, the pair reached the summit of the highest peak in the Alps. Balmat promptly traveled to Geneva to collect his prize money from de Saussure who, in turn, asked Balmat to organize his own ascent of the mountain. De Saussure succeeded the following year, at age 48, to reach the summit with Balmat as his principal guide. His success sparked the birth of mountaineering and broke the spell of fear and mystery that had enveloped the Alps until that day.

After this event, the valley of Chamonix and Mont Blanc became popular destinations for tourists and climbers alike. New routes and ascents on the more than 30 separate peaks over 12,000 feet were opened during the Golden Age of alpine mountaineering. Edward Whymper, the conqueror of the Matterhorn, made many first ascents in the Mont Blanc range, including the Aiguille Verte (13,524′) and Pointe Whymper on the Grandes Jorasses. Soon the main summits were climbed, and rock climbs of a much harder nature began to replace the easier snow ascents.

Aiguille Noire de Peuterey and Mont Blanc de Courmayeur

Alpinism came into its own with the founding of national alpine clubs: the Italian Alpine Club was formed in 1863, the French in 1874. In 1878 Clinton Dent made the first ascent of the Dru, and in 1892 another outstanding British climber, A. F. Mummery, made the first solo ascent of the Grépon in the Aiguilles de Chamonix, thereby inaugurating yet another era in mountain climbing. Of this achievement, Mummery would laconically say that it was "an inaccessible peak, the most difficult in the Alps, an easy outing for ladies." Speaking of the latter, the first two women to climb Mont Blanc to the summit were Marie Paradis of Chamonix in 1808 and Henriette d'Angeville, a French noblewoman, in 1838.

After Balmat, whose bold first ascent ranks as one of the more remarkable

Bionnassay Glacier
on Mont Blanc

achievements of the conquest and exploration of the Alps, and de Saussure, whose scientific high-altitude experiments on the summit of Mont Blanc opened the world of experimental science, and Edward Whymper, the passionate alpinist and artist, it is Mummery, the visionary, who by his outstanding climbs and unique book, *My Climbs in the Alps and Caucasus*, set the future course of grand alpinism by proclaiming the joys and pleasures of big-wall climbing.

From the 1920s onward, an ever-increasing number of alpinists have been drawn to the spires and rock walls of Mont Blanc, accomplishing numerous formidable ascents which rank to this day as some of the best climbs in the world. Suffice it to mention just a few outstanding feats and the men who performed them. There is the great solo climb of the Southwest Pillar of the Petit Dru by Walter Bonatti, a six-day solo epic that took place in 1955; the Red Sentinel and Route Major climbs of Graham Brown and Frank Smythe in 1927–28 on the Brenva Face of Mont Blanc; and the grand and classic north-face route of the 4,000-foot Walker Spur on the Grandes Jorasses by Riccardo Cassin and companions Gino Esposito and Ugo Tizzoni in 1938.

Mont Blanc can be reached by car, bus, or train. From Geneva, Chamonix is a mere three hours away. From Milan, half a day will get you to Courmayeur or Entrèves (a smaller and less crowded village at the very foot of Monte Bianco). These mountain towns have guide services where professional alpinists can be hired for the route one desires to climb. The Mont Blanc range abounds with mountain huts, many of which are equal to full-scale hotels. Wine, beer, good meals, and private rooms with bedding are available at some of these "huts." High-altitude cable cars criss-cross the mountain, enabling one to traverse the range without setting foot on snow. Chamonix and Entrèves are also linked by a seven-mile-long tunnel drilled under the venerable mountain itself, reducing car travel between France and Italy to a matter of minutes.

Matterhorn

Alps, Switzerland/Italy

The Golden Age of mountaineering, that romantic period in the 19th century (roughly between 1860 and 1890) when all the great peaks of the Alps were climbed for the first time, includes the first ascent of the famous Matterhorn (14,688′) by Edward Whymper in 1865.

"We started from Zermatt on the 13th of July, at half-past five, on a brilliant and perfectly cloudless morning," wrote Whymper in his classic book, *Scrambles Amongst the Alps*. "We were eight in number—Croz, old Peter and his two sons, Lord Francis Douglas, Hadow, Hudson and I. To ensure steady motion, one tourist and one native walked together. The youngest Taugwalder fell to my share, and the lad marched well, proud to be on the expedition and happy to show his powers. The wine-bags also fell to my lot to carry, and throughout the day, after each drink, I replenished them secretly with water, so that at the next halt they were found fuller than before! This was considered a good omen, and little short of miraculous."

Born in London in 1840, Whymper, a talented young engraver, was sent to the Alps by his publisher to prepare sketches of the most famous peaks. A year after his arrival on the continent in 1861, he made his first attempt on the Matterhorn, then the most desirable unclimbed peak in the Alps. He attempted the peak from Breuil, on the Italian side, which appeared to be the easiest side of the mountain. There he met Jean-Antoine Carrel, a native of the Val Tournanche; Whymper later described him as "the best cragman of his day." Whymper tried to hire Carrel as his guide (Carrel had made the first attempt on the peak in 1859) but was unsuccessful in his negotiations.

The Matterhorn, with villages of Breuil and Val Tournanche below

Overleaf: Breithorn Summit

Both started off independently, but neither man succeeded. Whymper was by now obsessed with climbing the Matterhorn. In 1862 he returned to Breuil and made five attempts; two were with Carrel and one was made solo! The relationship between the two men had meanwhile deteriorated, Whymper complaining that Carrel was unreliable and difficult to manage and that he considered outsiders attempting "his mountain" as "poachers." Carrel, on the other hand, was the best climber around and wanted very much to be the first to claim the Matterhorn, not only for Breuil and the Val Tournanche, but for Italy as well.

Right after Whymper's last attempt in 1862, the well-known English professor John Tyndall appeared in Breuil and hired Carrel from under Whymper's nose. Tyndall, who came well equipped with ladders and Swiss guides, reached higher than anyone before him but was stopped by a deep cleft below the final summit pyramid. Carrel refused to volunteer advice or give opinions, as he was hired only as a porter (moreover, the chief guide was Swiss, and he was Italian). Whymper, believing Tyndall's view that the mountain was unclimbable, left for London. He left his gear with the innkeeper in Breuil with instructions that it be given to any person who wanted to try again.

But he was back again in 1863, making yet another attempt over the same route with the same guide. This time a severe thunderstorm descended upon the party high on the mountain, and they retreated once again. He returned to London, "ready," he wrote, "to devise fresh combinations and to form new plans." In 1865 he returned with fresh plans not only for the Matterhorn but with an ambitious list of

peaks, among them the Dent Blanche (14,293′), Grandes Jorasses (13,806′), and the Aiguille Verte. This time he took the precaution of hiring his chief guide well in advance (in fact, a whole year ahead), and he was Michel Croz, not Carrel. Of Croz, Whymper had this to say, "Of all the guides with whom I traveled, Michel Croz was the man who was most after my heart." Croz, born in 1830, was ten years Whymper's senior.

On June 19, Whymper arrived in Zermatt to try another route—the southeast face. On the 20th, the party departed for Breuil via the Théodule Pass (10,883′), where they were joined by Meynet, a porter who was with him on previous trips. The southeast face proved to be too steep, with dangerous rockfall. Success still eluding him, Whymper returned once again to Breuil, but without his favorite guide, Michel Croz, who had a previous engagement in Chamonix. He found Carrel again and tried to talk him into the east face, but Carrel was unwilling to give up the old route. He finally agreed to go with Whymper, after the latter promised to try the old route again should they fail on the east face.

Whymper dismissed his guides. The following day Carrel found an excuse to escort some ladies to Aosta and detached himself from Whymper, who was left alone and guideless in Breuil. The next day the weather was bad and Whymper paced the inn at Breuil. He awoke the morning after to the news that a large party of guides had gone off to try the Matterhorn. On finding that Carrel was the leader, Whymper had a fit: "I felt bamboozled and humbugged." He quickly reasoned he might rush to Zermatt, try the east face, and beat them to it. This was easier said than done; there were no porters to carry his gear. But fate was on his side. At noon a party arrived from the Theodule Pass. It was Lord Francis Douglas, known to Whymper only by name. Douglas agreed to help Whymper get back to Zermatt and then to join him in a summit attempt. They crossed the pass on August 12, leaving their gear on Schwarzsee, including 600 feet of rope. They arrived in Zermatt and hired Peter Taugwalder. To their surprise, they met up with Michel Croz again. He was hired by Rev. Charles Hudson, who had come to Zermatt to attempt the Matterhorn. The Rev. Hudson and his friend Douglas Hadow agreed to join Whymper's party. Despite the desertion of Carrel, Whymper now saw a chance again and was determined to beat the Italians. They started off on the 13th and camped above the Hörnli Pass. The next day, finding few obstacles, they approached the summit, all the while wondering if the Italians were ahead of them. "The higher we rose, the more intense became the excitement," wrote Whymper. "What if we should be beaten at the last moment?" At last Whymper and his party reached the summit. They anxiously looked but found no footsteps in the snow. They were first! Looking down the Italian side, they saw Carrel 1,200 feet below. They yelled themselves hoarse and threw rocks at the Italians, who turned and fled. Yet Whymper felt regret at not having Carrel there with him, the man who "of all those who attempted the ascent of the Matterhorn most deserved to be the first upon its summit."

On the descent, tragedy struck. Four members of the party were pulled off by a slip of Mr. Hadow, and he, Douglas, Croz, and Hudson lost their lives. It was a shock from which Whymper never quite recovered.

Climbers on the lower Plateau Rosa

Tre Cime di Lavaredo

Dolomites, Italy

The Dolomites of northern Italy are among the most unusual and fascinating mountain ranges of the world even though they are not very high compared to the glacier-clad Himalaya or even as tall as the neighboring Alps (the highest peak, Marmolada, is 10,965 feet high).

The Dolomites are essentially large rock peaks that have little snow or ice. They are strange-looking, craggy, convoluted formations of limestone, often extraordinarily colored—ranging from pure white scree slopes, on which many of the peaks sit like pedestals, to yellow ridges and large walls of purple striations. The summits are ochre festooned with pink streaks. The limestone, known as "dolomite," named after its discoverer, the French geologist Dolomieu, is unique in that it is harder and displays more shades of coloring than ordinary limestone and contains magnesium as well as calcium.

The first peak to be climbed in this range was Monte Pelmo (10,394′) in 1857 by Sir John Ball, who also happened to be the first president of the illustrious Alpine Club of London. This climb heralded the beginning of Dolomite exploration and mountaineering, 70 years after the first ascent of Mont Blanc in the Alps.

Located in the northernmost corner of the Dolomites are the "Dolomiti di Sesto," which themselves subdivide into smaller formations of rock peaks. One such group is known as Tre Cime (three summits) di Lavaredo. While there are many large and impressive walls and peaks in the Dolomites—such as Civetta, Marmolada, and Monte Pelmo, none is more famous and awe-inspiring than the Lavaredo Massif. It displays a startling image of power and strength and is so monolithic yet well proportioned that it is difficult to estimate its enormous size.

Tre Cime di Lavaredo

Overleaf: Tre Cime di Lavaredo

This ultimate triad, with its Zen-like appearance (the towers remind me of the rocks in the Ryoanji temple of Kyoto) has not always been the peaceful scene it now is for the countless hikers, climbers, and tourists who drive to within a quarter mile from the Tre Cime. This area of South Tyrol was once part of the Austro-Hungarian Empire and the scene of intense battles between Italian and Austrian troops during World War I. The fighting not only raged in the deep valleys that surround the separate rock formations but also on the high ground. Some of the fiercest battles occurred near the Tre Cime, where individual rock towers were captured by troops trained in climbing techniques. The Cima Grande (the highest peak) was witness to a rather incredible (and somewhat comical) battle strategy. The Italians (never at a loss to come up with an expedient shortcut), at great risk and effort, hauled a huge spotlight and a hand-cranked dynamo to the summit of the Cima Grande by the easier back side—which they held. Then, on a particularly dark night, the spotlight was turned on, bathing the Austrian front lines in blinding light. The Italians charged and took the area by surprise.

After the war, Italy gained control of the South Tyrol. As a result, the lives of the German-speaking Tyroleans underwent a period of upheaval and turmoil—the worst years being those of forced deportation and/or resettlement under Benito Mussolini. A solution to the plight of the German-speaking population in South Tyrol was finally found in 1947 when the Italian government granted partial autonomy to

this region, known officially as Trentino-Alto Adige. Both Italian and German are now "official" languages. Streets, towns, mountain huts, even restaurant menus are given in Italian and German. In the region around the Tre Cime, German seems prevalent, perhaps because this area is closer to the border, with the larger German-speaking urban centers (such as Munich) immediately to the north. Today, the Dolomites are a popular tourist attraction not only in the summer but also in winter given their well-developed network of ski resorts.

After John Ball climbed Pelmo in 1857, the Golden Age, also known as the Classic Period, of Dolomite climbing began. The first man to climb the Cima Grande was Paul Grohmann, an Austrian surveyor and Dolomitic pioneer, who in 1869 climbed the south side with his friend Peter Salcher and the guide Franz Innerkofler. Grohmann was also one of the original founders of the Austrian Alpine Club, which began in 1862. By the time the Classic Period ended in the 1890s, all the big peaks had been climbed by their easiest routes, mostly by Italians, Austrians, Germans, and the British. Among the outstanding early rock climbers was Dr. Paul Preuss, who died in the mountains at the age of 27. He was a solitary and guideless climber, accomplishing, among other routes, the first ascent of the difficult Cima Piccola.

After the turn of the century, a new era of climbing began, that of the conquest of the big rock walls (some of which are over 4,000 vertical feet high) and other more difficult routes on peaks and spires. In 1909 Angelo Dibona made the first ascent of the northeast edge (Spigolo Dibona) of the Cima Grande with Emil Stubler. Then followed one of the first great feats of "superalpinism," Emil Solleder's climb of the west wall of the Civetta in 1925, followed by another, no less famous Dolomite climber, the great Emilio Comici from Trieste, who, with several others, in four days forged a route up the forbidding north wall of the Cima Grande, a face which up to

Lago di Landro, with Monte Piana in the background

Cima Piccola di Lavaredo

that time (1933) had been considered unconquerable. This was not only superalpinism but also the birth of *sesto grado*, or sixth grade, the hardest classification used by climbers, in which artificial aids, such as steel pitons, are inserted in the cracks to help the climber progress upward. Not satisfied with his exceptional conquest of the north face, Comici returned four years later and, in an incredible three hours and 45 minutes, achieved the first solo climb of the same route. Halfway up the face, and past the hardest pitch of the climb, he coiled his rope (solo climbers normally use ropes for protection, which they retrieve after every pitch by rappelling), gathered his pitons and carabiners and threw the whole lot down the face, where it landed more than 100 feet out from the base of the wall.

Thus came to an end the great modern period of Dolomite climbing. The peaks and crags of the Dolomites remain, however; to contemporary climbers, the north-facing, overhanging walls represent some of the ultimate challenges in rock climbing. The direct north-face route on the Cima Grande, for instance, is one of the great classic lines in the Dolomites.

Because the Dolomites are dotted with innumerable mountain huts serving the best of Italian and Tyrolean specialties, in the last 20 years they have become a paradise for the trail hiker and guided climber. They boast a network of high trails known as *via ferrata*, or iron roads, because of the extensive use of cables, ladders, and spikes strung along some of the most exposed ledgetrails to be found anywhere in the world. The Dolomites are truly a paradise for mountain lovers.

Mt. Elbrus

Caucasus, Soviet Union

The Caucasus, one of the world's great mountain ranges, stretch for more than 700 miles across the Soviet Union between the Black and the Caspian seas. To the south is Soviet Georgia, and beyond lie Turkey and Iran. As such, the Caucasus form a natural barrier between Europe and Asia and have influenced the political affairs of both continents since written history. These mountains have seen countless migrations, invasions, and counterinvasions. Prometheus is said to have been chained to rocky Mt. Kazbek, and the foothills have felt the feet of armies led by Turks, Tartars, Genghis Khan, and Tamerlane, as well as the more recent White Russians, Soviets, and Germans in World War II.

Mt. Elbrus

The Caucasus are dominated by Mt. Elbrus (18,481′), a sprawling, dormant volcano and the highest peak in Europe. Just six miles north of the main crest, Elbrus is located in the west-central section of the range, which also boasts the second, third, and fourth highest peaks in Europe—the granitic giants of Dych Tau (17,073′), Shkjara (17,064′), and Koshtan Tau (16,877′). Between these mountains stand hundreds of other precipitous peaks, including the so-called Matterhorn of the Caucasus, the notorious and difficult Ushba (15,449′). Below, vast glaciers and cascading streams lead down from the heavily wooded foothills into verdant valleys and gorges. Wildflowers grow in profusion right up to the icefields, strewing color through meadow and forest alike.

Historically, fierce nomads made the Caucasus unsafe for the casual mountain visitor. Today, the people of such independent Soviet republics as the Kabardinian-Balkarian Soviet S.S.R., who practice their Islamic religion freely, remain keenly aware of ancient traditions but welcome travelers from afar with warm hospitality, and the Caucasus have become one of the nation's most popular mountain recreation areas.

Training climb on nearby Mt. Cheget

The earliest climb on Mt. Elbrus is credited by Russian historians to Kilar Hashirov, a local peasant who, in 1829, guided a party from the Russian Academy of Science through the area and climbed the mountain's lower east peak with a companion, Akia Sottaev. In 1868 the pioneer British climber/explorer Douglas Freshfield came to the Baksan Valley at the foot of Elbrus and hired Sottaev to accompany him to the summit. Sottaev was then 80 years old! But he was far from finished with the challenge. Six years later, Britain's Grove expedition arrived and Sottaev joined up. He made the top of the west peak—higher than the east by 35 feet—to become, at age 86, the first man to have mastered both summits.

By 1905 detailed travel books were available, the range had been mapped, and

most of the significant peaks had been climbed. Almost every year witnessed new expeditions by teams from all over Europe, including such famous mountaineers as A. F. Mummery and the Italian mountain photographer Vittorio Sella, whose dramatic photos of peaks such as Ushba added greatly to the reputation of the Caucasus as a spectacular and intimidating range.

Doubtless, the Caucasus would still be considered one of the best places to climb and trek had World War II and subsequent East-West tensions not seriously restricted foreign travel everywhere in the Soviet Union. Fortunately, permission to visit the Caucasus and climb Mt. Elbrus is now relatively easy to obtain. The Soviet International Sports Committee (SOVINTERSPORT) operates mountain camps in the Caucasus (as well as in other regions of the U.S.S.R.), and foreign guests are welcome to buy a prearranged package.

Although technically easy to climb, Mt. Elbrus is a huge and demanding summit, with an ice surface of over 55 square miles and 77 glaciers that flow down the massive slopes. Crevasses, the potential for bad (and very cold) weather, altitude sickness, and white-out conditions are ever-present dangers that make this a noteworthy ascent.

Mt. Elbrus, west (left) and east summits

Travelers who wish to climb Elbrus must first proceed to Moscow, where all arrangements are made by Soviet officials, then fly to the city of Mineralye Vody, which is followed by a four-hour bus ride to the Baksan Valley and the Soviet mountain camp, called Azau (7,546′). From here it is a short walk to a cable car that lifts climbers, skiers, and tourists alike to Ice Base, at 12,467 feet. At last, one steps onto the snow and icefields of Elbrus. The route from Ice Base to the Priutt Hut can be covered in less than an hour-and-a-half. From the Priutt Hut—a comfortable shelter at 13,500 feet built in the shape of an Airstream trailer and offering room for at least 50 people—the route is straightforward to the saddle between the two summits. From the saddle, which can be reached in 6 to 10 hours, it is another hour or so to the east summit and a bit longer to the west peak, where a bust of Lenin looks out over the entire west-central Caucasus, from Dych Tau in the west, to Ushba, to Dongur-Orun (14,613′), and Nakra—a startling panorama of Europe's grandest heights.

Ararat

Turkey

If one were to ask the question, which are the three most famous mountains in the world?, the answers would most likely be Mt. Everest, the Matterhorn, and, no doubt, Mt. Ararat in Turkey. A very real yet near-mythical mountain, Ararat's name will forever be linked with the patriarch Noah and the ark. The story of Noah's ark, as told in the Bible, is an apparent reworking of a much earlier Babylonian tale, recorded in the Gilgamesh Epic (c. 2000 B.C.). It seems probable the story was based on an unusually devastating flood that swept the Euphrates River basin, wherein a large wooden ship was swept away and grounded on the high slopes of the Zagros mountains. Josephus (70 A.D.) and even Marco Polo (1300 A.D.) mention the existence of an ark on Ararat but add that their information is secondhand. Josephus also claims he was told that "its remains [the ark] are on display for all to see without the need for an organized expedition!"

The origin of the name Ararat comes from the Bible as well. The biblical text shows "r r t" with the vowels to be added. This means that "r r t" could as well be read as "Urartu," which actually was the name of an historic kingdom, with the ancient city of Van (100 miles from the old, now dormant volcano) as its center. Van became the capital of an Armenian kingdom founded by Tigranes the Great in the 1st century B.C., and there remains to this day a fine citadel in Van that dates to an early period in Armenian history.

At the base of Ararat live the Kurds. These people lead a nomadic life, migrating with their herds of cattle and sheep between the lower valleys and the high pastures where they live for three to four months every year. Here, in northeastern Anatolia, daily life has remained unchanged for centuries, and history speaks wherever one travels. Ancient Gregorian churches lie hidden in remote valleys, while interesting Ottoman mosques and 10th-century Christian monasteries—such as Sumela near Trebizond (today's Trabzon)—stand witness to a tumultuous cultural heritage.

Mt. Ararat

Ararat (16,946′) is an impressive, inspiring mountain, a sacred peak to Christians, and a mountain steeped in history and myth. Known to the Turks as Buyuk Agri Dagi, the peak rises abruptly in a single bulky mass near the Soviet/Iranian frontier of eastern Turkey. Ararat's slopes are made of black basalt, with the upper third permanently covered in snow. The last vertical 400 feet or so are ice.

Ararat was long considered unclimbable. One of the early references on scaling the peak regards the Shah of Persia, who offered a sum for the first man to climb it. Another early tale relates the story of the Pasha of Dogu Beyazit, the Turkish town nearest the mountain. One day the Pasha decided he would climb Ararat. He started off on horseback with a large retinue of servants but got only as far as his horse would carry him (about where the base camp is located today). In 1829 there appeared on the northern plain of Araxes a German traveler and scientist, Dr. Friedrich Parrot, who had come 2,300 miles from Dorpat University in Russia to conquer the sacred mountain. The erudite doctor, a fine mountaineer in his day, had first sighted Ararat from the summit of Kazbek, in the Caucasus, where he had been on an expedition 20 years before. "As I stood upon the Kazbek during a snow-storm," he wrote, "a momentary break in the clouds discovered in the distant south a high, round, solitary peak—in all

probability the silver crown of Ararat." When a peace treaty was signed between the Russian Emperor, the Tsarevich Constantine, and the Shah of Persia, Ararat became the extreme southerly boundary of the Russian Empire and accessible to Dr. Parrot. After gathering his team, his instruments, and his equipment, the intrepid Dr. Parrot set off for Ararat and began the first ascent. Finally, on October 9, 1829, they reached the summit. "I pressed forward," relates the doctor in his fine book *Journey to Ararat*, published in 1859, "round a projection of snow, and behold! before my eyes, now intoxicated with joy, lay the extreme cone, the highest pinnacle of Ararat." Five others made the ascent, among them Khachatur Abovian, the 20-year-old deacon of the local monastery, Alexei Sdrovenko and Matvei Chalpanof, Russian cossak escorts, as well as Ovannes Aivassian and Murat Pogossian, locals from the village of Arghuri. After pouring themselves a "libation [of wine] to the Patriarch Noah," the party descended from the summit, reaching the monastery of St. James two days later. Dr. Parrot wrote that he returned feeling as if he were "the Patriarch Noah with his sons, and with his wives, and with his sons' wives who, 4,000 years before, descended from Ararat."

Since that day, Ararat has been climbed many times—by German, British, French, Turkish, and American mountaineers, and many more from other countries. There also have been untold "ark hunters," publicity-seeking adventurers, charlatans, and writers bent on raking off some gain from the legend of the ark.

Until recently the mountain was under strict Turkish military control and out of bounds to all foreign climbers. The situation now has changed and as of 1984 mountaineers are once again permitted to climb the majestic biblical mountain.

The approach to the mountain is from the southwest. The road from Erzurum toward the Iranian border comes nearest to Ararat, at the drab, flat-roofed hamlet of Dogu Beyazit, the starting-off point for the climb. South of the present village is the old town, an ancient site, no doubt due to its location on the plateau. One of the more interesting archaeological sites here is the fortress-palace of Ishak Pasha. Today the standard ascent of Ararat requires about six days. A jeep track leads from Dogu Beyazit to Eli, where the trek to base camp begins. Camp I (13,800′) is reached on day two, Camp II (14,800′) on day three, then after another day at Camp II to acclimatize, the summit is gained on day five, with return to Camp II. On day six, climbers return to base camp and walk to roadhead.

For those who have stood close in Ararat's shadow, the mountain has worked its magic. Especially impressive from the north, where the plains of Araxes reach less than 3,000 feet, Ararat rises uninterrupted for nearly 14,000 feet, a vertical uplift that seems to have few equals in the world and that has held people spellbound since antiquity.

Above left:
Eastern Turkey

Above right:
Near Ararat,
in Eastern Turkey

Opposite:
Roman Arch,
Eastern Turkey

AFRICA

The continent with the least number of high mountains is certainly Africa. Here, the undisputed king of the continent is Kilimanjaro, followed closely by neighboring Mt. Kenya. The third highest massif in Africa is the cloud-shrouded Ruwenzori, the "Mountains of the Moon," on the border of Uganda and Zaire. While these African peaks are not among the highest nor most spectacular in the world, they are remote, exotic, and mysterious mountains, surrounded by deep forests, outsized vegetation, and fascinating legends.

In addition to this great mountain cluster of Kilimanjaro, Ruwenzori, and Mt. Kenya, Africa has a number of smaller ranges, such as the Atlas in the northwest, the Hoggar Mountains of southern Algeria, the Tibesti Mountains deep in the Chadian Sahara, and the great Rift escarpment along the eastern flank of the continent. My favorite mountains (besides Kilimanjaro) are Jbel Toubkal in Morocco (highest peak in North Africa), Mt. Sinai on the Sinai Peninsula, and the Hoggar rock peaks in the central Sahara. After climbing a number of these, I have also enjoyed the unique thrill of riding with camel caravans across the immense expanse of the salmon-pink sands of the Sahara to explore isolated and unknown ranges deep in the interior.

Berber mountain village, Atlas Mountains, Morocco

Once, after visiting the Tefedest Range, a subrange of granite domes and spires containing a large amount of prehistoric cave art, my friend Jean-Louis and I, together with our Tuareg guide, became separated from our pack train of donkeys and had to walk out across the hot dunes in one long do-or-die day, covering some 40-odd miles to the nearest village in a 13-hour nonstop march. As we struggled to survive the ordeal, without food or water, time slowed to a standstill. Mirage after mirage rose up from the endless sands, engulfing us in a mystical state of suspended animation. We had been walking since daybreak, with the lazing sun above and the muffled, grinding sounds of our Tuareg sandals on the bright orange sand. In the distance ahead, the fading ridges of Mt. Inoukoulmou took on a gentle haziness, preparing for the setting sun. We were getting nearer—my feet and calves ached terribly from walking in the bloody soft sand. All I could think about was finding hard sand surfaces—and water. "Hard sand, find hard sand." My whole world centered around these words. Hard sand made the walking just a little bit easier. Anxiously, I scouted ahead, carefully examining where I would put the next step. Smaller shadows in the scattered human and animal tracks indicated harder surfaces, except for camel tracks—they were useless as they hardly left any imprint at all!

Somewhere *soon*, I hoped, there must be a waterhole, a *guelta*, fed by some underground spring. The day was ending. Each step since dawn had been like a second of light. Thirty miles, perhaps ten hours. Nobody knew or cared, not yet anyway. Mountains and sand . . . mountains and sand. Silently we plodded on, thinking only of water and getting to the village of Mertoutek at the edge of the Tefedest Mountains. I thought of time long past, when this vast, endless desert had once been as lush and green as East Africa is today, and when lion, giraffe, wildebeest, and countless other game (depicted in the prehistoric carvings and

Above: South slope
of the Atlas Mountains,
Morocco

Left: Kilimanjaro,
below the Breach Wall,
Tanzania

Below: Sahara camel
expedition in Algeria

Above: Sinai
Mountains, Egypt

Right: Hiking toward
Shira Plateau on
Kilimanjaro, Tanzania

Below: Sunset on
Mt. Sinai, Egypt

paintings we had come to see) roamed these lands, now empty and reduced to sand and rock. High in the unknown Tefedest Mountains of the central Sahara, fragments of neolithic pottery, flints, arrowheads, and grindstones shimmered on rock slabs as if someone had left them there only hours ago. Everywhere there were mysterious and sensuous cave paintings and carvings of animals, their red-ochre and off-white tints a silent testimonial to skillful wandering artists of 6,000 years ago.

"*Aman, aman*," the quiet voice of our Tuareg guide roused me from my stupor. He pointed ahead and quickened his pace. I tried to speed up and follow but I had no strength. We had walked for nearly 40 miles. Suddenly it was there—a small pool of liquid diamonds, rippling and sparkling in the light of the setting sun. I reached for this glittering dance of lights and colors with my whole being. Staggering, but euphorically, I dunked my face. Warm, salty tears mingled with the cool, life-giving water. Kader Chelali laughed, a deep, warm belly laugh, exposing his badly decayed teeth. Kader, the magnificent nomad of the Sahara, knew the whereabouts of this waterhole. He took off his *seche* (turban), and for the first time I saw his full face and thick, black hair. He, too, succumbed to the seduction of the water. I cautioned him not to drink too quickly or too much. But he waved me aside and drank a bellyful. "You people care only about the paintings, but we Arabs of the desert have no use for them. We care only for green trees and water," he said with a broad grin. The village of Mertoutek was now close by. It was a small oasis with a few palm trees, some goats, camels, and small huts made of straw called *zeriba*. It had not rained for two years; the camels were too weak to ride and 60 goats were dead. There was no sugar, tobacco, or tea. Our arrival created a frenzy of activity. A dog barked, children ran around. The last visitors here had been a French archaeological group in 1935!

My legs felt like lead. Exhausted, we collapsed around a small fire in the darkness of Mertoutek. Someone opened a can of concentrated milk and poured it into a blue enameled bowl and added water. Twenty black-veiled Tuareg men joined us by the fire to observe us. They all talked at once. Dates were placed in front of us. "*Ekch, Amrar, ekch*" (Eat, man, eat!). Sweet, sugary dates, with watered-down cool milk—nothing *ever* tasted so good! And, slowly, life flowed back into my limbs.

In terms of major snow and ice climbing, Africa does not have much to offer. As a rule, most climbing is on volcanic rock and does not compare to the granite crags of the Alps, nor do the snow and ice of Kilimanjaro resemble what the giants of Asia offer. Nevertheless, some great routes can be found, notably on Kili's notorious Breach Wall, and several fine mixed alpine routes on Mt. Kenya. The Atlas has fairly good rock, but no permanent ice or snow. Snow appears only in winter and spring, when the central ranges near Marrakesh are popular with ski mountaineers—who climb the highest peak with sealskins attached to their skis, then make glorious untracked descents into the narrow valleys of the Berber villagers. Last year, Nadia and I made such a ski ascent—and descent—of that mountain with Omar, our Berber guide from Imlil, a remote hamlet nestled deep in a rocky gorge below Mt. Toubkal. Omar, 34, has a warm, infectious personality and a constant smile. He has that same type of easygoing *laissez-faire* attitude of the Tuareg of the Sahara. A guide for 16 years, married twice, he has six children by his second wife, Fatima. She's from the next village down the hill and—as is often the case with isolated mountain societies—is too closely blood-related to Omar. Two of their five boys are deformed—the oldest two have only a partial leg. They did not know

Summit ridge of Jbel Toubkal, Atlas Mountains, Morocco

about these things then, but they have enough children now, says Omar. When asked by Nadia if they planned to have more, he replied proudly, "My wife is on the pill."

We huffed up the trail from Imlil to Neltner Hut, a climbing refuge under the summit pyramid of Toubkal, built in 1934 by local Frenchmen. A donkey carried our packs and skis to the snowline at 9,000 feet. There we unloaded the animal and continued on by ski to the hut. There was a well-worn track in the snow, so I surmised that Toubkal must be popular. Indeed, the hut was a chaotic mess, packed to the rafters with German and Swiss climbers. The Swiss had just come down from climbing the mountain and had skied 4,000 vertical feet through three giant bowls, with inches of fresh powder over hardpack. Elated, they were busy celebrating. We couldn't wait to go! We were up and away by 7:00 A.M. This was mid-March in Morocco, the best time for a ski ascent of Toubkal. Omar said that he had not seen this much snow in 14 years—in fact, never in his entire life had there been so much of it. Not only had it snowed heavily along the entire Atlas, but it had rained in the south, where the Sahara is creeping up on the arable land. We started climbing—after the first 500 feet the slope steepened and became very icy. We could no longer proceed with our sealskins and had to insert *harsheisen* (German for ice-knives), a specially designed U-shaped toothed aluminum plate which is inserted between the ski boot and the binding and which functions as a crampon on the steep and hard snow. After four hours of laborious zig-zagging up the slopes and bowls of Toubkal, we finally emerged onto a small notch at 13,000 feet. The summit was not far off, yet the slope was quite steep and exposed, so we donned crampons for the last stretch to the

top. Finally on the summit, there was a fine 360° panorama of the central Atlas mountains, with the fertile lands and Berber villages visible in innumerable valleys below us. We savored the view for a long time, then returned to the notch where we packed our crampons, ripped the skins off our skis, locked our heels in the downhill mode and began a heady descent, skiing as far as we could, right to the snowline! Just there a couple of Berber porters happened to pass by on their way down, and for a small fee, they agreed to carry our skis to Imlil. We were happy with our success on Toubkal and celebrated with a feast of *tagine*, a meal of carrots, potatoes, and meat cooked in an earthen bowl, prepared by Fatima on our return. Flat loaves of bread and the favorite "*thé la menthe Berbre*" (Berber mint tea) completed the simple but delicious meal. Omar was happy. "Toubkal is our good fortune," he said. "So many climbers come here, our village is well off." He has done well also, and proudly showed us the small hotel he was building. I only hope he will continue to be a guide on his beloved mountain, where he is totally happy, and not get caught up in the mundane burden of running a hotel.

Jbel Toubkal

Atlas, Morocco

Climbers on the summit of Jbel Toubkal

According to legend, Atlas, the Greek giant whose shoulders supported the heavens, refused hospitality to Perseus and was metamorphosed into a mountain range. The Atlas Range of North Africa is indeed a gigantic—if broken—chain of mountains extending for over a thousand miles across Morocco, Algeria, and Tunisia. Most of the eastern half lies in Algeria and is high plateau country, with heights rarely exceeding 7,000 feet. The western part of the range has the high peaks, and all are located in Morocco. Here in succession are three waves of uplifts: the Anti-Atlas in the south, the High Atlas in the center, and the Middle Atlas to the north. The highest mountain of the High Atlas is Jbel Toubkal (13,671′), which also happens to be the highest peak in North Africa. Known to the Berbers who inhabit the high valleys surrounding the mountain as Adrar-n-Dern ("Mountain of Mountains"), Jbel Toubkal (*jbel* is Arabic for "mountain") is surrounded by somber but massive granite buttresses and rises as the king of the range, a scant 40 miles south of Marrakesh.

To those who perceive North Africa as being a barren and hot desert, the first glimpse of the High Atlas comes as a surprise, for upon arrival in Marrakesh, the imperial city of Morocco, one is immediately taken by a dazzling wall of snowy mountains, at least in winter and spring. Later in the season, the winter snows melt (there are no permanent glaciers) but in summer extensive snowfields do remain at the higher elevations on the northern slopes. The High Atlas effectively acts as a barrier between the fertile Mediterranean lands to the north and the scorching, golden sands of the Sahara, which stretch south for well over a thousand miles. Between Marrakesh and Toubkal lie the fertile plains of Haouz, enclosed by two highways that run south and traverse the Toubkal region. The eastern road crosses the mountains at the Tizi-n-Tichka (*tizi* means "pass") and the western highway passes over Tizi-n-Test. Both passes are about 7,000 feet in elevation, and it is possible (and eminently feasible) to undertake a lovely scenic drive, starting from Marrakesh and circling the highest peaks of North Africa—in only three days.

View of the
Atlas Mountains
from Marrakesh

The High Atlas is an ideal mountain region not only for the trekker and the climber but also for the ski mountaineer (ski mountaineers use downhill skis, touring bindings, and sealskins). The climate is comfortable, the approach to the mountains short, the Berber culture fascinating (a mixture of Hunza and Khumbu). There are mountain huts for climbers and skiers, plenty of guides, good trails, and mules to carry your gear. No wonder the High Atlas is popular with Europeans, who come here in large numbers, both in winter and summer. One of the more outstanding feats to accomplish here is the integral traverse of the best portion of the High Atlas, starting from the eastern approach road at Tizi-n-Tichka and ending the trip by returning via the western Tizi-n-Test pass. Many variations are possible, in winter as well as in summer.

The most active mountaineers have been the French, who climbed the major peaks before World War II. French expatriates in Morocco founded the French Alpine Club/Morocco section in 1922, the same year Toubkal was identified as the highest summit. Although the first recorded ascent was not made until a year later by the Marquis de Segonzac, it must be assumed that the summit of Toubkal was almost certainly reached before that date by local Berber tribesmen, as the climbing of the peak does not represent any technical difficulty. The origin of the name "toubkal" is unknown, but a Berber mountain guide suggested that the mountain had been named by the French after a certain "Monsieur Toubkal" who first climbed it. Besides de Segonzac, who was the leading French climber during the first three decades of the 20th century, other explorers such as Louis Gentil, Louis Neltner (who lent his name to the famous Neltner Hut at the base of Toubkal), and the Lepiney brothers were active before the war. A number of mountain huts or shelters have been built, of

Slopes of
Jbel Toubkal
above Neltner Hut

The south ridge of Toubkal, looking toward the Sahara Desert

which two are of interest to the Toubkal climber. One is the French Alpine Club hut at Imlil, the road's end and trailhead; the other, the Neltner Hut.

Many Berbers (who call themselves Shleuh) have become mountain guides and speak good French. They are a proud and fiery people, much like their Sahara cousins, the Tuareg, but they also have other traits similar to the friendly Sherpas of Nepal. A Berber guide therefore is not dissimilar (except for the language) from his Khumbu counterpart. Inhabitants of the High Atlas for thousands of years, the Berbers eke out a living from small-scale animal husbandry and agriculture. They grow walnuts, corn, and fruit. During the French conquest of Morocco, it was thc Berbers who offered the fiercest resistance until they were finally "pacified" in the mid-1930s.

A typical Berber village in the High Atlas consists of a cluster of 20 to 30 houses, flat-roofed and built of sun-baked mud, usually perched along a steep slope or rock outcrop overlooking the plains. These villages are inhabited by two, three, or sometimes four family groups. The women typically go unveiled, as opposed to their Arabic counterparts in the valleys below, and monogamy is practiced, in spite of the nominal Islamic rule that permits a man to have four wives.

The approach to Toubkal is by car from Marrakesh to Imlil. A paved road leads from Marrakesh to Asni (31 miles), then continues on a decent dirt road to Imlil, a Berber village at the head of the Mizane Valley. The trek begins here, with a hike along the upper Mizane canyon to the Neltner Hut. Toubkal can be climbed from this hut in one day.

Mt. Sinai

Sinai Peninsula, Egypt

Jbel Mussa ("Mountain of Moses"), Horeb, or Mt. Sinai—these are Moslem, Jewish, and Christian names for a summit that variously has been called the frontier of Heaven, the highest spiritual meeting place between man and God, the Mountain of God, the Magic Mountain.

On its summit God spoke to Moses: "You have seen what I did to the Egyptians, and how I bore you on eagles' wings and brought you to myself. Now therefore, if you will obey my voice and keep my covenant, you shall be my own possession among all peoples; for all the earth is mine, and you shall be to me a kingdom of priests and a holy nation" (Exodus 19:4-6).

Sinai Mountains above St. Catherine Monastery

Sunrise on Mt. Sinai

As legend has it, Moses fled Egypt after he killed a guard who beat a Hebrew slave. He escaped to the Sinai desert, where he roamed the mountains and the wilderness. In the Sinai he received the word of God from the burning bush, advising him to return to Egypt and free the Hebrew slaves. The slaves became Israelites and for 40 years wandered the Sinai desert. On their interminable journey they rested at a place called El Raha, at the foot of a mountain near where God had spoken to Moses from the burning bush. Located southwest of the plateau of El Tih, toward the tip of the Sinai wedge which pierces the Red Sea, there rises a jumbled array of dark brown granite peaks, their surfaces worn by wind and other forms of erosion. Among this cluster of peaks are Jbel Mussa (7,497′), Jbel Serbal (6,732′), Mt. Safsafa (7,112′) and Mt. Catherine (8,625′), the highest peak of the Sinai peninsula. Surrounding these mountains are two deserts, the Qa Ha to the south, descending toward Ras Mohammad (the Head of Mohammed), the tip of the peninsula, and the Sin desert to the north. According to biblical reconstruction, the Exodus route existed between the two deserts and among the mountains of Serbal, Sinai, and Catherine. It is at that time, c. 1300 B.C., that the Sinai became part of recorded history.

Mt. Sinai, with Mt. Catherine in the distance

After the Israelites camped at El Raha, Moses ascended a mountain where he again spoke with God. He remained there in a small cave just near the summit. Here God gave him the two stone tablets of the Covenant, the Ten Commandments. On his descent, Moses found the Israelites had reverted to their pagan rites and had made a golden calf. The event is commemorated today by a small chapel on a hill by Mt. Aaron, not far from the site of the burning bush, now the most sacred place inside St. Catherine monastery. The monastery was built in 530 A.D. by the emperor Justinian and later dedicated to St. Catherine, the virgin martyr of Alexandria, whose body was lifted by angels to the summit of the highest peak of Sinai, where monks subsequently discovered and collected a set of bones that they buried near the burning bush, inside the monastery.

To the local Bedouin, who call themselves Jbalaya ("the mountain people"), Mt. Sinai and the St. Catherine Monastery are a way of life, a *raison d'être*. They serve the monastery and the more than 20 Greek Orthodox monks who own the monastery and guide tourists around the area and up the mountain. The route to the summit follows a well-laid-out path of over 3,000 steps, zealously carved out of the granite by monks in the early centuries. The ascent is a good walk, gaining about 2,500 feet from the monastery's 5,000-foot elevation. While there are several routes, the most interesting path lies behind the monastery and ascends steeply toward a small green valley called Farsh Elijah ("Elijah's Valley"), where a number of small cells, ruins, and the prophet Elijah's small chapel are located. Here grow several large and ancient cypress

St. Catherine Monastery

Summit chapel on Mt. Sinai

trees, whose roots are watered by the springs of Sbahiya. To those who are so inclined, camping is possible here. From this vantage point, the remaining 1,000 feet to the summit are viewed head-on, and the red granite rocks, polished by the winds, take on magnificent hues. Before reaching this small valley, the large stone gate of St. Stephanos is passed. The gate is named for a 6th-century saint who took confessions here from pious pilgrims. Near the summit stands a small church, built of red granite blocks. The summit is close at hand, and on reaching it, one senses space and eternal existence.

Below, at the monastery, the monks who perform the tasks of the church go about their ways: meditating and researching and cataloging their incalculable treasures of ancient manuscripts, books, icons, and paintings—which have accumulated for over 17 centuries—while cultivating their spacious gardens adjacent to the 15-foot-thick walls of the monastery.

Mt. Sinai is not a spectacular peak, nor is it in any way a daunting or ominous presence. Indeed, it is a mountain of insignificance, a large outcrop among other, more imposing neighbors. According to the Jbalaya Bedouin legend, when word got out among the Sinai mountains that God was about to come down to earth to speak to Moses, all the surrounding peaks vied for attention and appealed to Him to be the chosen mountain. Only one small and insignificant mountain, Mt. Sinai, feeling unworthy of the great privilege, remained silent—which is why God chose it.

Today, after the temporary military occupation of the Sinai by Israel, the desert peninsula has been returned to the Egyptians. The region is now crossed by an asphalt road that traverses the peninsula from the Suez Canal to the east coast at Nuweiba, continuing to Elat, in Israel. Access by car is therefore easy from either direction. It is wise to plan a visit to this area around the days the monastery is open to the public (Friday and Sunday only, as of this writing). In addition to Mt. Sinai, the climb of Mt. Safsafa is recommended. Mt. Catherine is at present off-limits.

Hoggar Mountains

Central Sahara, Algeria

In the very heart of the vast and desolate expanse of the Sahara rise the spectacular Hoggar Mountains, a moonscape of towering basaltic spires and craggy pinnacles. Rising to nearly 10,000 feet—the highest peak is Tahat (9,573′)—the central core, known as the Atakor, is a composite of eroded volcanic crater plugs 100 miles in diameter. The scenery is powerful in the classic sense. Harsh, fragile, and timeless, it breaks the otherwise infinite orange haze of the flat and endless Sahara plateau.

Perched near the summit of Assekrem peak (8,950′), amid this vast desert of endless rock towers, stand a small chapel and a hermitage, built entirely by hand with stones gathered at random from the summit. This is the famous residence built in 1911 by Father Charles de Foucauld, a French army officer turned priest, missionary, and hermit. He spent the last years of his life here in meditation and prayer and laid the foundation for the Order of the Little Brothers of Jesus Christ, which his followers founded after his death. Ironically, his love of and caring for the impoverished and backward Tuareg tribespeople did not prevent his assassination at their hands when they overran the French Foreign Legion fort at Tamanrasset during the Tuareg/French war, which took place in 1916.

North face of Tezouiaig in the Hoggar Mountains

Although rock climbing is not unpopular in the Hoggar, the extremely dry climate and variable temperatures make for difficult and sometimes unpleasant experiences. Climbing ropes tend to fray, even melt, and the rock is not of the firmest variety. Nevertheless, important routes have been climbed on these desert spires by Europeans, who are attracted as much by the climbing as they are by the exotic location of their peaks. Among the more outstanding climbing opportunities of the Atakor are the Tezouiaig Needles, impressive spires that rise from the desert floor to over 9,000 feet. The highest, Tezouiaig North (9,055′) was first climbed in 1951 by the French team of Maurice Martin, Bernard Pierre, and Jean Syda. The other, Tezouiaig South (8,888′), fell to the Austrian party of Eduard Beyschlag and Hans Ellner as early as 1937. The French once sent a party of 58 climbers from the French Alpine Club; they climbed 50 new routes, made 250 ascents, and climbed 150,000 vertical feet. The Spanish and Italians also have been active in this area, putting up hard and direct routes on these peaks. Perhaps the best face climb is the west face of Tezouiaig South, which was made by the Spanish.

Visitors to the Hoggar come by way of Tamanrasset, the chief town in this part of southern Algeria—a huge country encompassing more than 900,000 square miles. Tamanrasset is also the gateway to points further south, including the forbidden Aïr Mountains, as well as to the wastelands of the Tenere, a rocky desert plateau devoid of even the smallest blade of grass for more than 300 square miles. (At one time there grew a single tree near a waterhole 100-feet deep—the tree was marked on the large-scale African maps but is now dead.) Today Tamanrasset, known to Algerians as "Tam," is a large oasis town lying at an altitude of 5,000 feet, about 60 miles south of the Hoggar Mountains. The town is reminiscent of an old Moroccan casbah, with low-built, mud-brown houses. Camels stand tethered by the tamarisk trees that line the dusty streets of this frontier town. Old crenellated mud ramparts of a former fort

Hoggar Mountain panorama, from the summit of Assekrem

remain—a lively and romantic picture evoking Beau Geste and the French Foreign Legion.

There is at present a fairly good four-wheel-drive track that leads from Tamanrasset to Assekrem and circles around the central core of the Hoggar peaks, which enables the visitor a quick visit to Assekrem (about three hours). A more interesting and rewarding journey is the trip entirely by camel, which avoids the jeep track altogether and takes six to seven days. Local Tuareg guides and camels should be booked in advance, however, as tourism is strictly controlled by the Algerian authorities, and on-the-spot travel arrangements for guides, food, camping gear, and camels are definitely not recommended. Once the party is confirmed and set to go, the trip ranks as among the most exotic and enjoyable desert experiences imaginable, especially for those who have never experienced desert travel before. The trail out of town leads along paths known only to the blue-veiled and mysterious Tuareg (most speak good French and occasionally some speak a few words of English) and up dry, rocky streambeds, called *oued*, north toward Assekrem. Camping under the stars allows one to fully appreciate the incomparable skies. While temperatures during the night

Above: Sahara Desert. Below: Camel expedition camp

plummet as low as 10° F (during which time a camp fire and generous portions of strong, sweet Tuareg tea keep one warm), they can shoot up to 100° or more during the noon hours. Travelers are advised to purchase and wear Tuareg-type clothing for their camel journey, including a turban (called *seche* by the Tuareg), a *gandura* (long, flowing robe), and a pair of hand-made leather sandals. There are occasional nomadic settlements en route, though one is never sure to encounter anyone. The Tuareg, being true nomads, move their *zeribas,* or straw huts, whenever new pastures for their camels are found. If a settlement or encampment is encountered, there usually ensues a *mechoui,* or local feast, replete with roast goat, couscous, and *tagela,* bread baked in the desert sand. The women then tie goat skins on the wooden urns, turning them into instant drums, which reverberate long into the night accompanied by song, hand-clapping, and dance.

After visiting the hermitage and the chapel high on the Assekrem, and perhaps having the unique experience of seeing the sunrise from the summit, one heads back to Tam with a fond farewell to the camels, the mountains, and the desert, as well as to the warm and friendly Tuareg, noble nomads of the desert.

Kilimanjaro

Tanzania, East Africa

In all of Africa no mountain has more mystique and popular appeal than Kilimanjaro, one of the largest dormant volcanoes in the world. The highest pinnacle of "the dark continent," the peak rises to 19,340 feet in majestic isolation, its ice- and snow-covered summit beckoning dreamlike above the surrounding game parks studded with animals. This is especially true when Kili—as it is often called—is viewed from Amboseli, Kenya's famous game park to the north. From here, the peak is often seen with a morning haze obscuring Kili's lower slopes, while high above the clouds float on the eternal snows of Kilimanjaro.

The earliest-known mention of snow on the equator dates back to the 1st century A.D. This is the story of Diogenes, a Greek merchant, who, on his way back to Greece from a journey along the East African coast, claimed to have traveled inland somewhere in Kenya, where, after a journey of some 25 days, he saw a "snowy range of mountains." The story was recorded at the time by the Syrian geographer Marinus of Tyre, and it was in part due to these writings that Ptolemy, the greatest astronomer

and geographer of his day, produced his famous map of Africa. On it the Nile River is shown to reach the equator, where lakes and a snowy range of mountains appear. Ptolemy's map remained an oddity for nearly 1,700 years, as during this time no one gave credence to the assertion that permanent snow could occur in the oppressive heat of equatorial East Africa. Then, in 1848, an English missionary visiting the interior saw "something remarkably white on the top of a high mountain" and proved Diogenes right. The report caused a sensation in British geographical circles in London, and for a time John Rebmann, England's hapless explorer and discoverer of Kilimanjaro, was discredited. Eventually other pioneers reached the mountain and confirmed Rebmann's sighting, but it was not until 14 years later that anyone made an attempt to set foot on the mountain. Another five years were to pass before anyone reached the snow on the saddle between Kibo, the central and highest cone of Kilimanjaro, and Mawenzi, a subsidiary peak (16,893′).

The Breach Wall of Kilimanjaro

Overleaf: Wildebeest in Amboseli Game Reserve below Kilimanjaro

Kilimanjaro was eventually climbed 100 years ago by Hans Meyer, a Leipzig geographer, accompanied by his Austrian guide, Ludwig Purtscheller. After barely reaching the rim of Kibo's mile-wide summit crater, the determined German returned three days later from his high camp below to once again climb the rim and circle over

to reach the highest pinnacle, which lies about 700 feet higher on the opposite side. This summital point of Africa he named Kaiser Wilhelm Spitze in honor of the German Emperor, for it was the highest point not only in Africa but in the entire German Empire. (Germany had recently annexed a large part of East Africa, known as Tanganyika.) The summit peak has since been renamed Uhuru Point (meaning "freedom" in Swahili) by the Tanzanian government when that country was formed in 1964.

There are many fine routes on Kilimanjaro, for either hiking or trekking, as well as a number of moderate and difficult climbs of a technical nature. There are at present five major trails, of which the most popular and no doubt easiest is the so-called Tourist Route, which starts from the various hotels at Marangu, a town to the southwest. Mountain huts along the way provide food and shelter (check current conditions at the hotels) and the climb is usually made in five to six days. And while many reach Gilman's Point, on the southern rim, fewer have the stamina and the desire to continue to Uhuru Point.

Machame Trekking Route on Kilimanjaro

Other trek routes are the Mweka Route from the town of Moshi and the village of Mweka at 6,000 feet, where a direct track leads up along a forested ridge to just below the summit cone. There is also the Umbwe Route from Lyamungu that leads to the Barranco Hut near the Great Barranco, a large gash in the side of Kibo. Here one has the option of either following the Arrow Glacier Route up the Western Breach (a spectacular though somewhat technical route), or traversing east to connect with the upper end of the Umbwe Route. Both of these routes are little used and are recommended for especially adventurous trekkers. Another route from the north starts at

Kilimanjaro rim,
Rebman Glacier

Loitokitok, in Kenya, but travel along this trail is at present not permitted as the border must be crossed and there is no checkpoint. Finally, there remains the beautiful Machame Traverse Route. Departing from the hamlet of Machame, one traverses the entire mountain via the Shira Plateau, the Western Breach and the Breach Wall, the Great Barranco with its fabulous forest of giant groundsels, lobelias, and heather, and the hanging Heim Glacier. Then one heads up to Stella Point, climbing scree slopes between two small glaciers, and across the rim to Uhuru. The route continues down to Gilman's Point and then via the Tourist Route to Kibo Hut, 5,000 feet below, and back along the regular route on the sixth day to Marangu, where a fine hotel with good fare awaits.

Of the many technical climbing routes on Kibo, the southern glaciers offer the finest challenges. Here one can find multiday climbs on the Decken, Kersten, and Heim glaciers, all of which involve the use of an ice axe, crampons, and ice pitons. One of the most difficult climbing problems of the mountain is the Breach Wall, a 4,000-foot-high rampart of steep ice and crumbling rock, nearly a mile-and-a-half wide. This huge face, considered the most imposing mountain wall in Africa, has two high-angle glaciers: the Balletto Glacier below and the hanging Diamond Glacier high above it, separated by a vertical section of rock, down which enormous icicles hang like wax drippings from a candle. Several parties have tried to climb the most prominent of these icicles—the one, in fact, that connects the two glaciers—but have failed in their attempt. It was not until Reinhold Messner appeared on the scene in 1978 that the icicle was climbed, thus establishing the most difficult route on Kilimanjaro and no doubt in all of Africa.

ASIA

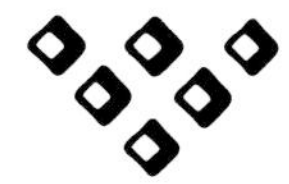

The vertical geography of Asia's dramatic great Himalayan uplift is the product of plate tectonics: the crashing of the Indian subcontinent into the Asiatic mainland. For here rise the Himalaya and the Karakoram, two of the world's most awesome mountain chains embracing the highest peaks on earth. In addition to these Cyclopean-sized mountains, Asia has scores of other ranges, some unnamed and unexplored by Westerners to this day, with most of them possessing many peaks of 20,000 feet or more. Placed in Africa or North America, these "unknown" mountains would constitute sizable and memorable mountain terrain of major importance.

But the mountains of Asia are more than just big, spectacular, and numerous. Many of the highest summits are also revered by the local people as godlike beings, Sacred Thones and givers of the Eternal Life. Some are worshipped as the Center of the Earth by millions of Hindu and Buddhist devotees. While other cultures also revere mountains as sacred—Asia has by no means the monopoly on mountain worship—expressions of piety are more pronounced and in evidence here, especially in Tibet, Bhutan, Nepal, and India, where Hindus and Buddhists predominate.

My favorite mountain regions in these exotic lands are the high deserts of Ladakh and Zanskar (also known as Little Tibet) in northern India, the central highlands north of the Karakoram Range in China's Sinkiang province, and the incomparable Khumbu region of the Sherpa people in eastern Nepal, which sports the most astounding concentration of high mountains on earth.

Naltar Peak in Hunza Valley, Western Karakoram, Pakistan

Asian mountains require expeditions. Climbing trips to big peaks are serious and complex undertakings. They are also tedious, long, drawn-out affairs that require months, even years, of planning. Long approach marches and siege tactics are the norm. Traditional expeditions involve lots of people (both climbers and porters) and often are expensive. What's it like to be a member of a big expedition? Once in base camp, the climber spends 80% of the time sitting around waiting for something to happen, 10% taking action when something finally does, and 10% experiencing terror—from snow avalanches, hidden crevasses, fierce storms, and treacherous ice slopes, not to mention exhaustion, the rarefied air, and the subzero cold at high altitude.

But the experience can also include good cheer, companionship, and merrymaking with the indigenous people, as the night we celebrated the anniversary of the "People's Liberation" in the small Tibetan village of Liu Baxiang, at the base of Minya Konka, during a mountain climbing expedition I organized in 1980. It was October 1, the People's Republic National Day. That night, before setting off for the mountain, the local Tibetans gave us a rousing send-off party replete with generous libations of rakshi, and song and dance performed by the young girls of Liu Baxiang, whose shuffle dance was not dissimilar to the slow shuffle of the Sherpas of Nepal.

Three days later we set up base camp near the Konka Gompa, a ruined Buddhist tem-

Unclimbed "Lady Finger" near Naltar, Hunza, Western Karakoram, Pakistan

ple built at the foot of the mountain, wantonly destroyed by the Red Guards during the Cultural Revolution. I took photos of what remained of the sacred paintings: a Buddhist Wheel of Life, a half-destroyed image of the saint Guru Padma Sambhava. That night it snowed hard. Confined to base camp with a bout of pneumonia, I became the base manager, responsible for shipping off loads with our team of Tibetan porters to the advance camps on the mountain.

It had been snowing incessantly, but as soon as the weather cleared, the scene outside my tent was awesome, for Minya Konka filled up the entire view. The larch trees were turning color and the rhododendrons looked forlorn under the snow. A Himalayan blood pheasant strolled shyly by my tent. The valley was incredibly beautiful, pristine, and wild, a Shangri-La. The Tibetans were friendly and took turns keeping us company. All carried rosaries and/or prayerwheels, reciting their sacred mantra "*Om Mani Padme Hum*"—"ode to the jewel in the lotus," over and over the whole day long. I felt very happy here, happier than I ever could be back home in California.

I remember a particularly fine morning that dawned clear. Deciding to go for a hike, I took off up a long rocky ridge above the Gompa (known as Rock's Ridge) and climbed to 15,000 feet to where a series of moss-covered chorten (religious rock towers) overlooked the valley. Above me loomed the incredible summit pyramid of Minya Konka, considered the most beautiful mountain in China, while far below numerous glaciers flowed into deep, forested valleys. By noon clouds were starting to gather—I wanted to climb higher, to reach a spectacular viewpoint from where Joseph Rock photographed Minya Konka for the National

Advance Base Camp on Batura Glacier, Hunza, Pakistan

Overleaf: On Siachen Glacier, Eastern Karakoram, India

Geographic more than 50 years ago, but my lungs could no longer breathe the cold, thin air, and I had to descend.

It rained all that night, complete with thunder and lightning. It was impossible to sleep, yet I felt happy here at base camp below the mountain. This feeling of blissfulness, combined with the peaceful isolation and grandiose scenery, gave me a feeling of guilt, which became reflected in a quote from Albert Camus that I jotted in my diary: "No doubt that I was suspect of living fully, with free abandonment to happiness . . . this is unforgivable." Soon after I wrote this, my snug little expedition world fell apart.

At 6:00 P.M. we had radio contact with Camp II. High on the mountain, disaster had struck—there had been an avalanche and four climbers had fallen 1,500 feet down the mountain. Jonathan, a television network cameraman, had been killed and two others, among them my good friend Kim, were injured.

I was stunned. Just at that moment, a new stormfront hit Minya Konka—bedlam ensued. I tried to coordinate the radio messages that were flooding in, relaying them to the respective camps. I immediately started negotiations with the Chinese officials to obtain a helicopter. They said it would be impossible and would take a month! A self-rescue was organized.

The next morning Clark and I decided to go up to Advance Base Camp to assess the situation: an all-day climb. On arrival at the camp we found everyone had come down off the mountain. Kim had been diagnosed with a broken back and was in excruciating pain. Dick,

Hawk, Sia Kangri, and Broad Peak, Siachen Glacier, Eastern Karakoram, Pakistan

our doctor, had wrapped him as tightly as possible in a foam mattress, and despite heavy doses of morphine, he had moaned the whole night long. Yvon, also in the avalanche, had several broken ribs and a possible concussion, and was oblivious to his surroundings.

The others were all in their bags, dazed, pale, and haggard. All except Dick wanted to leave. The risks of climbing further were too high. Conditions on Minya Konka were now impossible due to the extremely high avalanche danger from the latest heavy snowfall. Eventually, all agreed that the climbing route was dangerous. We moved out, the helpful porters carrying Kim on a makeshift stretcher in relay teams.

Jonathan was buried on the mountain with Buddhist rites offered by his friend Rick. The expedition was over. Dorje Lutru, the Thunder God of Minya Konka, had won this one.

In 1986 I again had the opportunity to organize a climbing expedition in Asia, this one being a joint Indo-American attempt on Sia Kangri, a magnificent 24,300-foot mountain in the heart of the Karakoram Range. Tucked far back at the end of the Siachen Glacier, longest in Asia, the mountain rises on a disputed border between Pakistan and India, in what in fact turned out to be a war zone. The Siachen Glacier, 48 miles long, constitutes the eastern approach to the mountain and had never been traversed in its entirety by a Western party. It was an approach necessitating eight high camps (more than are used on a climb of Mt. Everest), and was entirely on the 1,000-foot-thick ice of the Siachen, flowing down some of the most rugged terrain in the world.

The idea of climbing Sia Kangri was appealing to me, for it meant that we would be

traveling across some remote mountains, while traversing the forbidding and high ranges of northern Ladakh. We would also be crossing central Asian rivers with such exotic names as the Indus, the Shyok, and the Nubra, to reach our base camp at the foot of the Siachen Glacier.

Tapovan, Shivling base camp, Garwhal, India

Overleaf: Mt. Ratabam, Garwhal Himalaya, India

Our party of seven Westerners and seven Indian mountaineers assembled in Leh, the capital of Ladakh, a medieval city located at an elevation of 12,000 feet and only recently opened to foreign tourists. While the expedition did some last-minute shopping, I paid a visit to the regional army commander to clear permission for our short-wave radios and to set up emergency rescue procedures. The Indian army had agreed to provide transport to our base camp, and two days later our convoy set off from Leh towards the intimidating Kardung La (18,300′), the highest known road pass in the world. On the icy windswept pass we stopped our caravan briefly to offer prayers at a small Hindu temple, the intense cold and strong gusty winds causing us to move on quickly. Descending the other side, we entered the Nubra district of Ladakh, an area that had been closed to tourists and foreigners for over 50 years. Six thousand feet below us flowed the mighty Shyok River, an upper tributary of the Indus. I no longer had the feeling of being in India or even in Little Tibet . . . this definitely looked and felt like the deep and barren riverine valleys of Yarkand and Shaksgam, of what is now Chinese Turkestan, where I traveled in 1983.

After an interminable 14-hour jolting ride in an army jeep over the worst dirt road imaginable, we stopped for the night in Panamik, halfway up the Nubra Valley. This was also

the village where we had previously arranged to pick up our team of 40 porters, which we would need to carry our equipment to our Advance Base Camp below Sia Kangri. Panamik, a sleepy, pastoral village, was extensively terraced with well-tended fields of barley, corn, and beans. Large clumps of wild roses (*Rosa webbiana*) grew profusely along the roads. The houses were a mixture of traditional Tibetan-style and Ladakhi architecture. Many had open verandahs with large corner windows facing south. Not having seen Westerners here for decades, the villagers were shy and most hid from view.

After one more day "on the road" we arrived at last at our base camp near the terminus of the Siachen Glacier—ten days after leaving the United States. Snow flurries were gently falling and it felt like winter, although it was the middle of July. After repacking and sorting out loads for our porters, we were off onto the ice by mid-morning of the third day.

Unclimbed rock peaks, Batura Muztag, Western Karakoram, Pakistan

Four hours later, we reached Camp I in a blinding snowstorm. We were now at 14,000 feet, and I had to struggle with numb fingers to erect my tent. It was quite a tough start, yet the next morning was clear, calm, and promised to be hot. The combination of high-altitude radiation and reflected sunlight on the glacier ice can create terrific heat. By noon the temperature was into the high 80s. The porters labored under their loads but seemed oblivious to the heat. I concluded that having lived in the Nubra all their lives, they had adapted to the altitude and the high desert summer heat rather well.

As we proceeded to the next camp, we occasionally had to cross ice gullies of meltwater; some could be jumped but others were 10 feet wide and as many feet deep—in some

Sunset on the north face of Mt. Everest, Tibet/Nepal

places the meltwater had carved gashes 50 feet deep into the ice! Aluminum ladders had been brought along for crossing these scary and often intimidating streams. The bravest of us walked across the ladders standing up, while the not-so-brave (including me) preferred to crawl on all fours!

Two days later we were at last on firm snow, having reached the 16,000-foot level. At about noon I spotted a porter carrying a bundle of skis on his back, and as I caught up with him I saw he had mine in his load. So out they came and on they went. Soon the entire team got on skis and proceeded up the glacier in this fashion to our Advance Base Camp at 18,000 feet.

The scenery at Advance Base Camp below Sia Kangri was spectacular, with unclimbed 23,000- to 24,000-foot peaks thrusting all around us. Then again, without much warning, a storm struck. Our small camp, forlorn and isolated in the snow, became a dark speck on a vast tableau of turbulent violence, and for the first time a feeling of utter loss and loneliness swept over me. For three days the storm raged, pinning us inside our tents. Then the front moved on and the actual climbing was ready to begin. Suddenly the crashing sound of an explosion reached us, and then another—in panic we rushed about our tents. We were being shelled by heavy artillery! Pakistan, in conflict with India over ownership of the glacier and adjacent mountains, was telling us in no uncertain terms to keep out! Misled by assurances of safe conduct, our party of Westerners decided to forgo the slopes of Sia Kangri and instead skied to the highest Karakoram passes ever stood on by Americans—Indira Col (18,898′) and

Turkestan La (19,210′), both on the line of control between India and Pakistan but sheltered and well away from the line of fire. The Indians, however, decided to do the Sia Kangri climb and successfully reached the summit, returning six days later. Fortunately, no one was injured.

After we were reunited at our Advance Base Camp, we quickly evacuated to a safer location, descending to Camp V. Here at last we felt secure and celebrated our various victories with the personnel of the Indian army outpost. Then time came to return to the base camp at the foot of the glacier and head home. Travel was made difficult by the many crevasses and near-impassable ice gullies filled with meltwater. On day 37, after more than five

Himalayan panorama with Mt. Everest (center), looking northeast, Nepal/Tibet

weeks on the ice of the Siachen, we walked off the glacier onto level ground and were able to relax, the continuous and ever-present danger of hidden crevasses or sinkholes off our minds. It had been a tough expedition—the altitude, the shelling, the dangerous terrain—everyone looked ten years older. Often, on the glacier, my teammates and I would wake up from nightmares or an inability to breathe, panicked with the possibility of contracting pulmonary edema, that feared and often fatal illness that besets climbers at high altitudes. But now we could rest in the shade of flowering pink tamarisk among the meadows below the glacier. Then someone managed to expropriate two cases of beer from the army supply depot, and we knew at that moment that we were back in the land of the living! Some expedition!

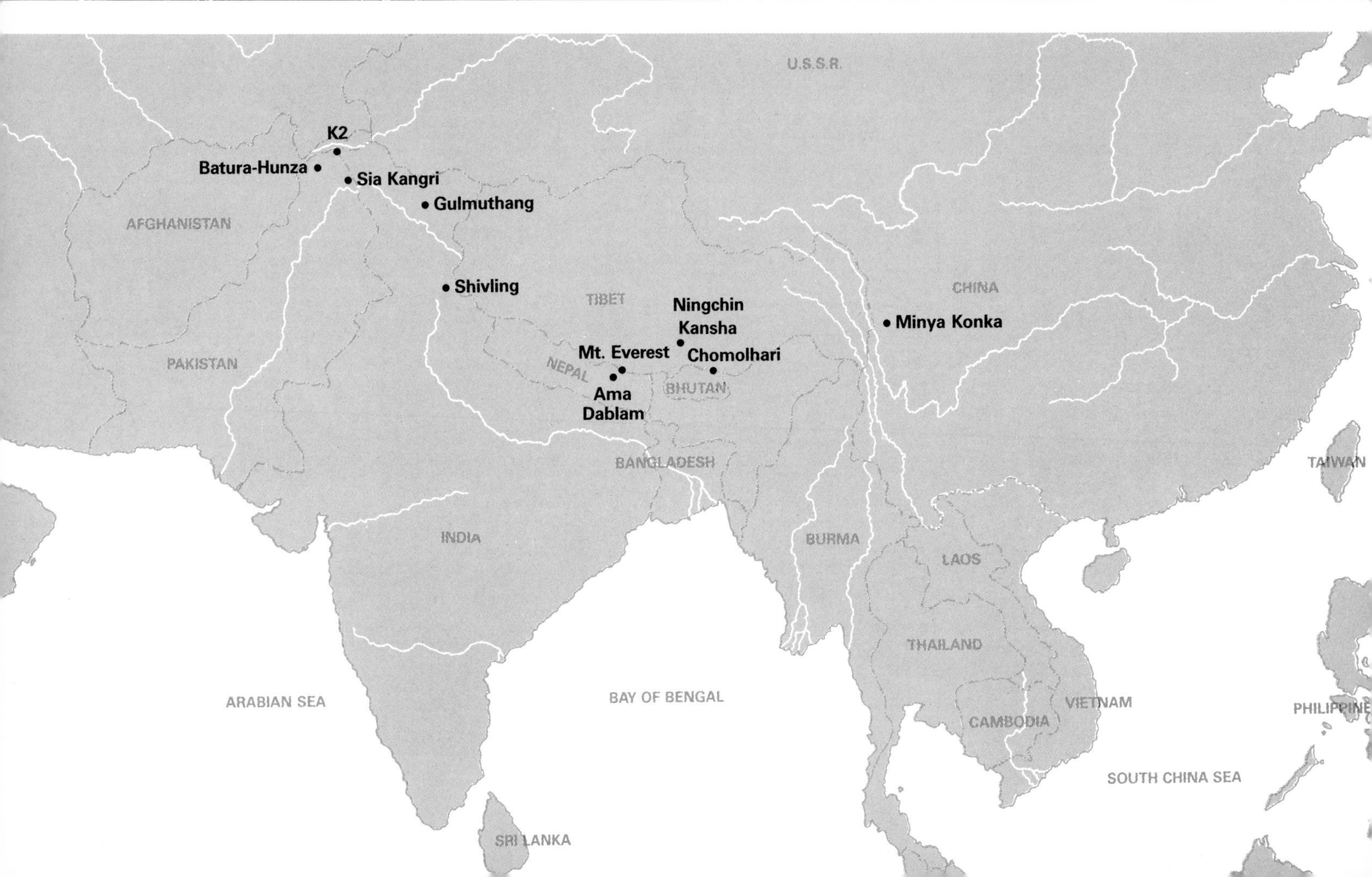

U.S.S.R.
K2
Batura-Hunza
Sia Kangri
Gulmuthang
AFGHANISTAN
Shivling
TIBET
Ningchin
Kansha
CHINA
Minya Konka
Mt. Everest
Chomolhari
PAKISTAN
NEPAL
BHUTAN
Ama
Dablam
BANGLADESH
TAIWAN
INDIA
BURMA
LAOS
THAILAND
ARABIAN SEA
BAY OF BENGAL
VIETNAM
CAMBODIA
PHILIPPINE
SOUTH CHINA SEA
SRI LANKA

Batura-Hunza

Western Karakoram, Pakistan

The mountain Shangri-la of Hunza, in the western Karakoram of Pakistan, is one of the finest alpine environments on earth. Here one can find gigantic ice-clad peaks, precipitous valleys, and wild mountain torrents. Set amid these natural wonders are the picturesque villages of the Hunza people. Hunza is part of the vast northernmost region of Pakistan, known as the NFD, or Northern Frontier District. From the village of Gilgit (a small but important nerve center) to the Chinese border and the Wakhan corridor of Afghanistan, Hunza is bound on all sides by large mountains. East of Hunza lies the central Karakoram with giants K2, Gasherbrum I, Broad Peak, and Gasherbrum II—the four "eight thousanders" of Pakistan (only about 14 mountains on earth are higher than 8,000 meters, or 26,247 feet).

Batura icefall

Overleaf:
Batura Peaks and
Batura Glacier

The peaks of Hunza are easily accessible—the new Karakoram Highway now snakes its way through the heart of the Hunza Valley toward the Khunjerab Pass (16,200′) that leads into China—and they are hardly lower than their gigantic cousins to the east. The highest Hunza peak proper is Distaghil Sar (25,870′), while Rakaposhi (25,551′) is no doubt the most spectacular peak of the region. This mountain, a major landmark of the Hunza Valley, rises steeply for nearly 19,000 feet above the highway. It is a breathtaking scene of overpowering grandeur to see this enormous yet elegant mountain from the highway below.

Hunza is indeed a land of superlatives, not only for its mountains, valleys, and rivers but also for its people, the famous Hunzakuts, known for their longevity (some individuals are said to have reached the age of 140!). Their leader, the Mir, formerly an absolute ruler, is now the titular heir to the Hunza realm only, although he still maintains a sizable castle in Baltit, the regional capital nestled in the center of this ancient kingdom. In 1974 Prime Minister Bhutto merged Hunza into Pakistan, thus ending 900 years of Mir rule. The present Mir, Gazanfar Ali Khan, is an elected member of the National Assembly and lives with his wife and three sons in Islamabad most of the time. Two separate ethnic groups live in Hunza, the Guichos and the Bruchos. The Guichos are Wakhi people who live in Upper Hunza (Passu, Gulmit, Chapursan,

On the Batura Glacier

Batura), while the Bruchos live in central and southern Hunza. "Brucho" derives from the language Brucheski, the original Hunza tongue. The Bruchos are also the original inhabitants and are said to be descendants of Alexander the Great's army, as so many have fair complexions and blue eyes. The Guichos of the north are darker and originally came from Afghanistan or as far away as Turkey. The Wakhi tongue, called Guvicheski, is similar to the Wakhi spoken in Afghanistan. Lower in Hunza, people also speak the Chenaki dialect, a mixture of Aryan and Sanskrit.

Opposite above: Passu Peaks and Batura Glacier

Opposite below: Porters on the Batura Glacier

In the northernmost region of Hunza rises what amounts to the last major uplift of the Karakoram Range, the Batura Mustagh, a heavily glaciated region of high mountain escarpments, large glaciers, and stupendous steep icefalls. Here the immense Batura Glacier flows for 37 miles from the Kampire Dior (23,435′) to the confluence with the Hunza River. One of the longest rivers of ice in Asia (only the Siachen and the Baltoro glaciers rival it for length, size, and spectacle), the glacier lies at the northern foot of the Batura escarpment, a 25-mile-long flank of ice the size of which is unique in the world. This wall of ice comprises no less than 26 points rising over 22,000 feet, while the glacier flows serenely 10,000 feet below. The highest peak, Batura I (25,570′), was first climbed in 1976 by a German expedition led by Dr. Alexander Schlee. A previous attempt on the very difficult and dangerous icefall of this peak ended in tragedy when five members of an Anglo/German team disappeared en route to their high camp in 1959. This icefall, one of the longest and most massive in the world, tumbles more than 13,000 vertical feet from the upper levels to the glacier below. The second-highest peak, Batura II (25,466′), was climbed in 1978 by a Japanese party.

The Batura was not visited until 1925, when a party of Dutch explorers led by Charles Visser investigated the entire length of the glacier. They reached several high passes at the head of the Batura, as well as two passes to the north, which they hoped to traverse and explore beyond. This area, known as Lupghar and Chapursan, eluded them, however, as they were forced to retreat due to low food supplies, as well as the unpredictability of the unknown glacial terrain. In 1985 I led an expedition to the same area, with the intent of crossing the same pass Visser climbed in 1925 and exploring the Lupghar Valley, but permission was denied by Pakistani authorities at the last moment.

For the tough mountain traveler, the Batura region offers some of the finest exploratory trekking in the world. As for alpinists on the lookout for unclimbed peaks to conquer, the Batura Karakoram has plenty to offer. Less than six of the region's 20 peaks over 22,000 feet have been climbed.

K2

Karakoram, Pakistan/China

Hidden deep inside the Karakoram mountains on the border of Pakistan and the Chinese province of Sinkiang, and thus not visible from any inhabited village in either country, stands K2, the world's second-highest mountain. The Karakoram is a spectacular range of highly glaciated peaks, generally considered part of the Great Himalayan Range, even though they are separated by the deep trough of the Indus River Valley. Much smaller in length than the Himalaya, the Karakoram nevertheless embraces four of the earth's 14 peaks that stand over 8,000 meters in height (approximately 26,250 feet). The mightiest among them is K2, a savage, steep, and isolated pyramid that many climbers consider the most difficult high peak anywhere—and definitely harder than Everest.

To the people who live near it, in both Pakistan and China, the pinnacle is known as Chogori ("Great Mountain" in Urdu). It was first seen by Western eyes in 1856—by a member of the Survey of India party at a vantage point from the south in Kashmir. Lieutenant T. G. Montgomerie, who had struggled up a 16,000-foot peak with a heavy surveyor's theodolite, described his discovery thus: "Beyond came the snowy points of the Karakoram Range and behind them I saw two fine peaks standing very high above the general range." He took bearings and designated the apparently taller summit K1, the lesser one K2. When the peaks were surveyed three years later, K1 was found to be closer and lower—about 25,600 feet. K2, on the other hand, is now calculated at 28,250 feet (though the government of Pakistan claims to have surveyed it at 28,741 feet). Thus, while Montgomerie's humble designation remains as its name, K2 comes within several hundred feet of being the loftiest peak in the world.

The peaks of the Karakoram

Lieutenant Francis Younghusband, a young British officer, was the first European to glimpse K2 from the north during his epic journey in 1887, when he traversed the length of China, crossed the Karakoram, and reached Delhi—an eight-month trek.

K2's summit towers 12,000 feet above Concordia, a wide glacial expanse at the head of the Baltoro Glacier, the standard route of approach from the south, or Pakistani, side. The massive bulk of this giant peak is equally intimidating from the north, where it can be seen from the K2 Glacier, 16,000 vertical feet below.

Reaching the heart of the Karakoram is no easy matter from any side. The Baltoro approach is a tough but dazzling two-week trek to the traditional base camp at Concordia. Those who attempt this journey must be hardy and experienced adventurers, accustomed to walking over rough, trail-less terrain containing loose boulders and slippery glaciers. The approach from the north is somewhat shorter and easier. From the roadhead at Mazar Dara, which is reached after three days of dirt-road travel from Kashgar, the trek takes a week to reach the base camp at Suget Jangal. K2 is so elusive that even from here the mountain cannot be seen. It takes at least one more day of travel to reach the K2 Glacier, where, at last, Chogori reveals its magnificence.

To say that such a splendid mountain would cast a spell on man's desire to reach for its very pinnacle would be an understatement. K2 has been an obsession for climbers since the beginning of the 20th century when the first expedition, led by the notorious demonologist, Aleister Crowley, attempted the peak, approaching it via Skardu and Askole and the Baltoro Glacier. And this obsession has lasted to this day.

The mountain has been an especially strong magnet not only for the Italians—

who made the first ascent—but also for the Americans, who sent a team to K2 in 1938, and who made two more determined attempts to be the first on top—in 1939 and 1953. None of these expeditions were successful. It remained for the Italians Achille Compagnoni and Lino Lacedelli to make the first ascent, on July 31, 1954.

K2 was not attempted from the north until 1982, when the Chinese Mountaineering Association (for a rumored sum of $1 million) gave permission to a Japanese team to attempt the north ridge. From Kashgar, a bazaar of Turkic and Uygur Muslims and the westernmost city in China, the expedition drove for three days along the southern fringes of the vast Takla Makan Desert, including a crossing of the Kun Lun Mountains by way of a 16,000-foot pass and a harrowing descent into the Yarkand Valley, where their 300 load-carrying camels had been assembled at the roadhead. After crossing the Aghil Mountains, they reached Suget Jangal in six days of trekking, set up Advance Base Camp at the foot of K2 under the imposing and gigantic sweep of the north face, and reached the summit along the north ridge. One climber fell to his death on the descent.

K2 Glacier, with K2 in the background

Overleaf: Along the Shaksgam River Valley, Karakoram

K2 has now been climbed by many different routes, no fewer than 20 expeditions have been mounted in the past few years. But the toll in lives lost has been terrible. In 1986, violent storms caught many climbers of various expeditions by surprise while they were high on the mountain; 13 died. Nevertheless, new generations of mountaineers will continue to be obsessed with K2, and no doubt the extreme objective dangers of this mountain—avalanches, storms, high altitude, and steep, technical, icy terrain—will continue to serve as an ultimate test of the human will.

To visit K2 from Pakistan, fly to Gilgit, in the Northern Frontier District. Bus to Skardu and jeep to the roadhead at Askole, then trek along the Baltoro Glacier to Concordia and back—approximately 25 days of arduous trekking.

To reach K2 from China, fly to Kashgar via Urumchi, in western China, then travel by road (three days) to Mazar Dara roadhead. From there, trek to base camp in one week. Allow six more days to visit the amphitheater at the base of the north face of K2, and return. The walk out requires six days, but the return drive can be done in two.

Sia Kangri

Eastern Karakoram, India/Pakistan

Sia Kangri, the "Rose Peak" (24,350′), stands guard over the Siachen Glacier, longest glacier in the world outside the subpolar regions. Culminating on the borders of India, China, and Pakistan, Sia Kangri is part of the Karakoram Range, the second-highest mountain range on earth. The Karakoram is separated from the Great Himalayan Range by the Indus River and the intervening Ladakh Mountains. While considerably shorter in distance than the Himalaya (the Karakoram is only one-sixth the length of its large cousin to the south), the 250-mile range is a true continental divide, with all precipitation north of the crest flowing into China and what comes down on the southern flank flowing either into Pakistan or India.

At present, the Siachen Glacier, as well as Sia Kangri and other large mountains along the Karakoram crest, are disputed territory, claimed by both India and Pakistan. Geographically, the area is part of Ladakh, also known as "Little Tibet," and the people are Buddhists. A large number of whitewashed monasteries and *gompas* (temples) dot the Ladakhi landscape, not only across the wide Indus Valley but also in the Nubra Valley, where the Siachen Glacier flowed during the Ice Age. Once ruled by kings, Ladakh is now part of the Indian state of Jammu and Kashmir; the land was conquered by the Dogra rulers of Jammu in 1834. Four mountain ranges punctuate the arid Ladakh moonscape: the Himalaya to the south (which acts as an effective rain shadow, preventing monsoon clouds from penetrating to the high plateau beyond), the Zanskar Range, the Ladakh Range, and the Karakoram.

The Hawk,
Siachen Glacier

The Siachen Glacier, which provides access to the icy inner world of the Karakoram, is a majestic expanse of ice 50 miles long and 3 miles wide. The glacier originates on Indira Col (20,866′), on the border with China, north of Sia Kangri. From this watershed pass, the Siachen flows evenly and straight for 35 miles, encased to the south by the Saltoro Range, a major Karakoram spur, and on the northern side by the easternmost crest of the Karakoram. Further down, the glacier makes a dogleg turn around the rocky spur of the Terong Mountains and ends at 12,000 feet, where the meltwaters come gushing out of the glacier to give birth to the full-fledged Nubra River. The stream, dark green in color, is powerful and flows down the U-shaped Nubra Valley—carved by prehistoric ice—to the junction with the Shyok River. The Nubra Valley today is home to a dozen Ladakh villages. Fields are terraced, irrigated, and well-tended, and barley, corn, beans, and other green vegetables appear in sharp contrast to the dull brown earthen surroundings. Clumps of fragrant wild roses grow profusely along the road and in the villages beneath the wooden houses of the Nubra people. Nubra homes are built in a mixed style of traditional Tibetan and Ladakhi architecture. Many have the typical Ladakhi wooden veranda with corner windows facing south to take advantage of the warming sun.

The Siachen Glacier was discovered by Dr. Tom Longstaff (see chapter on Mt. Assiniboine) in 1909 after he crossed the Saltoro Pass (now Bilafond La) from the south. A well-known British explorer and climber, Longstaff studied maps given to him by his father and had become curious about an apparent blank area. Determined to discover what the unexplained spot was, he traveled to India to resolve the mystery, despite a prestigious invitation by Robert Falcon Scott to join him on his expedition to the South Pole.

On the
Siachen Glacier

Many more parties visited the Siachen after Longstaff, most noteworthy of which was Fanny Bullock-Workman's expedition of 1911, which carried out extensive surveys on the upper Siachen and named both the Indira Col as well as Turkestan La (19,210′), another pass at the head of the glacier that leads to Chinese Turkestan. After the explorers came the climbers, and in 1934 a large international expedition under Professor Gunther Dyhrenfurth made the first ascent of Queen Mary Peak, the name given by Mrs. Workman to the mountain now known as Sia Kangri. Since that time, Sia Kangri has become quite popular, with ascents from the Pakistani as well as from the Indian side. One of the last private parties to travel here, before border skirmishes broke out in 1984, was the amazing ski expedition of Ned Gillette and Galen Rowell, who skied from the mid-Siachen across the south face of Sia Kangri and down the Baltoro, Biafo, and Hispar glaciers, an unsupported journey of 400 miles across the icy roof of Asia.

Opposite above:
Nubra Valley,
Eastern Karakoram

Opposite below:
Siachen Glacier
and Eastern
Karakoram,
from Indira Col,
India/Pakistan

The approach to Nubra Valley and the Siachen is by way of Leh, capital of Ladakh. Special permits are currently required to travel to Nubra due to the hostilities. The road linking Leh with Nubra traverses the Khardung La (18,350′), highest road pass (and one of the most perilous) in the world. The road plunges precipitously from the top, down the far side into the deep, V-shaped canyon of the Shyok River, a major tributary of the Indus. The track follows the stream until it reaches the confluence with the Nubra River. Here an ancient cable suspension bridge spans a narrow gorge, and the traveler enters the Nubra Valley, once the summer residence of the kings of Ladakh. The wide riverbed and the deep, oversized rocky canyons devoid of snow or vegetation are more akin to the stark, vast landscapes of central Asia, not those of the Indian subcontinent. Once the snout of the Siachen is reached—a full day's drive along a rough mountain track built for army vehicles—the approach to Sia Kangri can begin. The journey is best accomplished on skis, with camps on the glacier. The final camp is set at 20,000 feet near Conway saddle. Far above lies the summit of Sia Kangri, a mountain that also gives birth to the ice of the Baltoro Glacier, which flows toward Hunza in Pakistan. Other major peaks on the junction of these two glaciers are Gasherbrum I, the world's 11th highest peak (26,470′), the white pyramid of Chogolisa (25,148′), and Baltoro Kangri (23,990′—also known as the Golden Throne). Other giants of the Karakoram, which can be seen from the Siachen icefields, are Saltoro Kangri (25,400′), Mt. Ghent (24,281′), Singhi Kangri (25,430′), Teram Kangri (24,491′), and the unclimbed Hawk, an ice pyramid with a sharp, crooked summit (22,160′).

Gulmuthang

Zanskar, Himalaya, India

Lost among the vast desert ranges of southern Ladakh lies a 1,000-year-old feudal kingdom called Zanskar, "Land of White Copper." High, dry, and semi-barren, Zanskar lies hidden between the folds of the Zanskar peaks and the Great Himalayan Range, the most awesome mountain range in the world. It is here, among these ice-clad desert peaks of the Zanskar Mountains that one finds Gulmuthang (20,570′), a glaciated peak of impressive design. Also known as Z-3, the mountain was first climbed in 1913 by an Italian party led by Mario Piacenza, who called it "Cima Italia!" The second ascent was not made until 70 years later, when Zanskar was opened again to the West.

Although the mountain rises above the head of the Durung Drung Glacier and dominates the western escarpment of Zanskar, it is technically part of the Himalayan Range. There are other, larger peaks near Gulmuthang, such as Sickle Moon (21,568′) and Brammah (21,050′), but these form part of the Kishtwar Range, which adjoins Zanskar to the west. Gulmuthang is the most outstanding peak in view as one reaches the high Pensi La (14,439′), which allows entry into Zanskar from Baltistan and the Suru Valley.

Once ruled by two kings, Zanskar is a land that stretches across the infinity of time. It is ignored by most Indians and unknown to most of the outside world. The people of Zanskar, like their Ladakhi cousins to the north, are Tibetan Buddhists. White-washed *gompas* (temples) cling to rocky bluffs in the mountain heights, while in the valleys learned monks and nuns pass on the teachings of the ancient Tibetan masters. Here, in this magical land, every peak and river is the dwelling place of a god or goddess, demon or fairy, and good-natured superstition influences much of daily life, as it did in Europe during the Middle Ages.

Gulmuthang, from Pensi La

Traveling by road from Kashmir, climbers and trekkers bound for Zanskar drive to Kargil, where one usually spends the night. The following day one can drive along the famous Suru Valley, which leads to the Pensi La and Zanskar. The end of the Suru is marked by a 1,000-year-old monastery, Ramdung Gompa, active to this day.

Once over and across the Pensi La, the road quickly descends to the upper Doda Valley, one of four principal valleys of Zanskar. At the bottom of the pass, those who have their eye on Gulmuthang can set up a base camp near the tongue of the Durung Drung Glacier, which is within a stone's throw of the road. From here an easy trek route leads along the west side of the glacier to the foot of the mountain. Camp I can then be set up near the base and the glacier crossed at this point.

For those who wish to visit the inner valleys of Zanskar, the road descends along the Doda River past several villages. The ancient Buddhist monasteries in Zanskar are well worth an in-depth visit, and, before reaching Padum, there is the pastoral complex of Sani with its ancient cottonwood trees and garden—an oasis in an otherwise parched desert landscape. A famous European scholar, Csoma de Koros, was the first white man to visit Zanskar; in the 19th century he resided here, working on the first book of Tibetan studies. Further down the river is the sprawling Karsha Monastery, the largest and most important in Zanskar. At the end of the motorable road is Padum, an unattractive administrative center for the Indian government that is inhabited by about 600 people, half Zanskaris and the other half Muslim merchants and traders from Kashmir.

The people and the mountains of Zanskar offer a truly unique experience for the adventurous traveler as well as for the mountaineer looking for a different cultural experience and spectacular mountain scenery. Life is hard in Zanskar, but the beauty of the desert, the friendly people, and the magnificent and active monasteries are well worth the price of the harsh sun, dusty roads, and arid countryside.

Descending Bardar Glacier, Zanskar Himalaya

In the
Chenab Valley,
Indian Himalaya

Shivling

Garwhal, Himalaya, India

The mountains of Garwhal are India's finest Himalayan peaks. A relatively compact area, no more than 175 miles long, this superb cluster of mountains stretches from the Nela Pass in the west to the Kali River in the east, the border between India and Nepal. Here, among precipitious gorges, roaring streams, flower-filled mountain meadows, and villages set amid dense pine forests, rises the Matterhorn of India, the awe-inspiring Shivling (21,467′).

Shivling

Overleaf:
Baghirati Peaks I, II, and III, Garwhal Himalaya

The area was heavily visited by British climbers and explorers prior to World War II; Nepal then became forbidden territory for Westerners. Famous climbers such as Shipton, Smythe, Meade, and Longstaff fill books written about Garwhal. These intrepid Englishmen explored the deep gorges around Nanda Devi, scouted approaches to Kamet on the Tibetan border, and surveyed most of the difficult Garwhal terrain over a period of less than 40 years.

The highest peaks, Nanda Devi (25,645′) and Kamet (25,446′), were first climbed in 1936 and 1931, respectively, while Trisul (23,360′), the first 7,000-meter peak climbed, had fallen as early as 1907 to the experienced mountaineer Tom Longstaff. Shivling itself was climbed in 1974 by two Indians, Hukan and Laxman Singh, assisted by four Sherpa guides.

To the devout Hindu, however, Garwhal is much more than a challenging mountain destination. Here, among the mysterious and forbidden mist-shrouded crags and near impenetrable river gorges, the legends and myths of Hindu mythology were born and still thrive. The mountains of Garwhal are the traditional abode of the Hindu deities: Vishnu the Preserver, Shiva the Destroyer, and Rama, the incarnation of Vishnu. They also have names of religious origin: Nanda Devi is Kali, Trisul is Shiva's trident, and Shivling represents Shiva's phallus.

Left: Gaumukh, source of the Ganges River, Garwhal Himalaya

Below: Pilgrims at Gangotri, Garwhal Himalaya

Opposite: Shivling, above Tapovan

Just below the fish-tailed summit of Shivling, with its stark vertical walls of sheer granite, the long Gangotri Glacier comes to an end and a sacred stream is born. This is Gaumukh, the cow's mouth, the ultimate destination of every devout Hindu—a site as holy to Hindus as Mecca is to every Moslem. In fact, the Baghirati River, which flows out of an impressive and constantly cracking ice-wall, is considered to be the real source of the Ganges River, the mother of India. Thousands of pilgrims every year struggle to reach this place and bathe stoically in the stream's icy waters in the belief that all sins will be washed away. Among the pilgrims, many sadhus or holy men, who have made the long journey from southern India dressed only in a saffron cloth around their waist and carrying a metal bucket for offerings, sit in meditating postures facing the mountains.

Truly a remote region, the Garwhal is little known to foreigners. Traveling by bus or car to Gangotri, a holy site for pilgrims and the start of the trek to Gaumukh, is no easy task. The narrow road is often in poor repair, and on occasion the downright hair-raising turns, mudslides, and exposed passages make the journey a perilous one for the unwary. At Gangotri, where the Baghirati shrine erected in the 18th century marks the end of the road journey, the traveler can at last relax and enjoy a spectacular waterfall and gorge, beautiful pine forests, and walking trails. A beehive of activity, Gangotri is unique. Pilgrims camp along the road, others wash their clothes and themselves in the icy stream nearby, while enterprising merchants sit behind rows of stalls selling assortments of trinkets, amulets, charms, and offerings to the gods. At dark crowds gather inside the temple for a candle-lit ceremony and a procession accompanied by loud chanting.

For those who wish to trek to the glacier, the easy journey can be made in two or three days. Above Gaumukh, the terrain steepens considerably until it opens up into a beautiful meadow known as Tapovan, or place for meditation. Traditionally all expeditions to Shivling have set up their base camp here sharing the beauty of the surrounding peaks and the little flowers by the stream with a few hardy followers of Shiva who spend their summers meditating in small caves.

Minya Konka

Hengduan Mountains, China

"There is no more beautiful spot on earth than Minya Konka. One night spent on the mountain is equivalent to sitting ten years in meditation." So declared an ancient Buddhist inscription that explorer Joseph Rock remembered reading when he first visited the Konka Gompa temple in western China, located at the foot of Minya Konka, China's highest mountain (24,790′). An early traveler in China's Yunnan and Sichuan provinces, Rock was on assignment for the National Geographic Society when he explored the Konka Longba Valley that led up to Minya Konka and the 600-year-old Buddhist temple located below the mountain. Here he mapped, measured, and photographed the area, took bearings on the peak, and became convinced that he had discovered the highest mountain in the world. In February of 1930 he thus wired the society with his proposed elevation—30,250′! This was certainly an astounding figure for no mountain on earth—then or now—surpassed the 30,000-foot mark. The society rightfully refused to believe him, but rumors started and a great deal of excitement began stirring in the mountaineering world by the possibility, no matter how remote, that a peak higher than Everest might exist somewhere in the unknown interior of western China. It was enough to motivate four young Americans, who set off on an expedition to Minya Konka the next year. Crossing all of China, a journey which took nearly a year, they succeeded not only in finding the peak and exploring its various faces and ridges but also in making the first ascent. The summit was reached in 1932 by Richard Burdsall and Terris Moore. It was one of the major achievements of the time, considering the size of the party and the extensive explorations that were carried out. As a result, Minya Konka remained the highest peak climbed by Americans for 26 years thereafter. In 1956 the Chinese, under the leadership of Shi Zhanchun, the present chairman of the Chinese Mountaineering Association, made the second ascent, but not without casualties, as four climbers were lost on the upper slopes of the mountain. The third party to attempt Minya Konka was again an American team, organized by myself in 1980, and was the first group of Westerners to approach Minya Konka since 1932. Unfortunately, the expedition ended in tragedy when a member of the film crew fell to his death during an avalanche set off by the lead climbers on the descent from Camp II to Camp I.

Minya Konka from Rock's Ridge

There have been numerous expeditions to Minya Konka and the Hengduan Mountains of western Sichuan since, some with tragic results. A Japanese team of 25 members from Hokkaido attempted the mountain in 1981 from the east side for the first time. Starting from the Yan Tsoko Valley and glacier, a party of eight neared the summit when the lead climber, unroped, slipped and fell to his death down the north face. The remaining seven gave up their summit bid and descended—now roped!—but after downclimbing for only 200 feet, another climber slipped, pulling all remaining six in the party with him down the precipitous north face to their deaths. In the same year, a Swiss party approached the mountain from the east side as well and set up base in the Hailoko valley, from where they made successful first ascents of no less than six peaks over 6,000 meters (19,685′), among them Sun Yat Sen Peak (22,593′), the second-highest peak in the range, after Minya Konka.

Above: Near Kanding, Hengduan Mountains

Below: Yuelongshi Valley, Hengduan Mountains

Minya Konka from Tshumi La

Access to Minya Konka is difficult at best. The only practical approach is via Kanding, an ancient Tibetan gateway city previously known as Tatsienlu. From this fair-sized town, where one can buy most staple foodstuffs as well as camping utensils, etc., there are several routes to the mountains from which to choose. One is via the Sichuan-Tibet Highway, which crosses the 14,000-foot Thseto La pass onto the Tibetan upland, then goes south along the Litschi River to Liu Baxiang, a small commune of Minya Tibetans and the end of the motorable road. From here it's a three-day trek to reach the base camp at the Konka Gompa. Another approach is via Yue Ling, a hamlet five miles south of Kanding, from where a trail starts that connects the Djezi

La pass (15,650′) with the Yuelongshi Valley, meeting the Liu Baxiang route on its second day. The Yue Ling trek is longer, requiring about seven days, but the route is more scenic and little used and offers some of the finest trekking in all of China. The area has never been logged, and there are no roads into the Hengduan Mountains. Wildlife is abundant and the luxuriant vegetation is rare. The only downside is generally poor weather as this region suffers from extensive monsoon rains and cold winter months. The only window of good weather appears to be October/November. The mountains of the Hengduan Range are spectacular, however, and offer never-to-be-forgotten splendor to those who come in search of them.

Mt. Everest

Himalaya, Nepal/Tibet (China)

To see the big Himalayan mountain giants up close is the thrill of a lifetime. To bask in the presence of Mt. Everest, the highest of them all, is an event all by itself. Everest dwarfs the other giants around it and stands supreme as the reigning monarch of the Himalaya. George Leigh Mallory, the mountaineer famous for his offhand explanation of why he wanted to climb Everest—"because it is there"—expressed in more lyrical terms the awe that Everest evokes when he contemplated the mountain from the Kangshung Valley of Tibet in 1921: "Mount Everest above us was immanent, vast, incalculable—no fleeting apparition of elusive dream-form: nothing could have been more set and permanent, steadfast like Keats' star, 'in lone splendour hung aloft the night,' a watcher of all the nights, diffusing, it seemed universally, an exalted radiance."

From 1938 to 1950 Everest was impossible to approach, as the kingdom of Nepal, on whose border with Tibet the mountain is located, would not open its frontiers to tourists, and Tibet, on the northern side of the Himalayan crest, was declared off-limits to the outside world from the beginning of World War II until 1980 by the government of the People's Republic of China. With the growth of trekking and adventure travel, it is now possible for all who so desire to pay a visit to the mountain king, either by trekking from the Khumbu district of east Nepal or by crossing Tibet by truck or bus to the base camp in the Rongbuk Valley. Here one can see Chomolungma, as Everest is called by the Tibetans, from less than ten miles away, with nothing to interrupt the view of the broad north face, which rises a vertical 10,000 feet into thin air to culminate in the pinnacle of the earth at 29,028 feet.

Mt. Everest from Rongbuk Valley, with religious tablet

Overleaf: North face of Mt. Everest

Mt. Everest was discovered by the West in 1852 during a geographical survey conducted by the British while in India and was named after its surveyor-general, Sir George Everest. But the Tibetans, on the other side, had known about it for a much longer time. The name Chomolungma means "Mother Goddess of the Earth," indicating that the Tibetans intrinsically understood this mountain to be the most awesome in the world. Modern science, redundantly, proved them right.

As a mountaineering objective, Everest has had more than its share of expeditions challenge its dizzying heights. As of 1987 more than 150 climbers, including six women, have stood on its summit, savoring one of mountaineering's greatest victories. The oldest was Dick Bass, an American who reached the top in 1985 at the age of 54. While the first ascent took place via the South Col route in 1953—climbed by the New Zealander Sir Edmund Hillary with Sherpa Tenzing Norgay—many climbing routes have been established since. There are now routes on the south, west, and north sides of the peak, as well as a difficult new eastern route, the Kangshung Face, established by an American expedition led by Jim Morrissey in 1983. Besides the Americans, who have been very active on Everest (Tom Hornbein and Willi Unsoeld were the first Americans to climb the west side and descend by the south), the Japanese, Chinese, British, Soviets, Australians, and French, among others, also have reached the summit.

Scaling Everest, of course, has not been without casualties. The mountain has one of the highest death rates of any peak in the world. By current estimate, approxi-

mately 100 people have perished. The greatest dangers have been avalanches, falls in crevasses, cold, and the effects of the thin air, causing a condition known as pulmonary edema, which can be fatal unless the victim is brought to lower elevation rapidly. The slightest slip on rock or ice can bring death on Everest. Sherpa guide Ang Phu, after successfully climbing Everest twice, fell backward off a small stance in the snow and was unable to check his 7,000-foot fall down the northwest face.

The Sherpas, a race of tough mountain people who inhabit the southern slopes of Mt. Everest, have been pillars of strength on Everest expeditions, traditionally carrying the heavy loads and bottled oxygen, often to a height of 25,000 feet or more. Most climbers who attempt Everest use oxygen to diminish the effects of thin air at high altitude. However, it has become somewhat fashionable to make oxygen-less ascents since 1978 when it was first done by the world's premier mountain climber, Reinhold Messner, together with partner Peter Habeler. Messner also holds the record for the first solo climb of Everest, which he did in 1980 from the Tibetan side, along the North Col route.

Ruins of Shegar Monastery

Pilgrims near
Ganden Monastery,
Lhasa Valley

Despite its difficulty and the fact that the mountain has been climbed by so many people along so many routes, the ascent of Mt. Everest remains one of the most sought-after mountaineering objectives in the world. Indeed, the permits required by the Nepalese and Chinese governments are difficult to obtain, with waitlists extending into the mid-1990s on both sides.

To get to Everest from Nepal, trek from Kathmandu to the district of Khumbu in east Nepal and on to the base of the mountain—a journey of about 20 days. Or fly in to the small mountain airstrip of Lukla in Khumbu, and save about 14 days. Walk out from the base to Lukla in 4 or 5 days. To get to Everest from Tibet, go by truck, jeep, or bus from Lhasa, capital of Tibet, or drive from Kathmandu via the Nepal/Tibet border road to Shekar, then over the Pang La. Either route leads into the 17,500-foot high Rongbuk Valley, at the foot of the Rongbuk Glacier that descends from Everest.

Ama Dablam

Khumbu Himalaya, Nepal

The Khumbu region of eastern Nepal, that vertical battleground of rock and ice where the Indian subcontinent collided eons ago with the Asiatic mainland, is one of the Great Himalayan Range's most awesome places. Here Everest, Lhotse, Cho Oyu, Nuptse, and scores of other Himalayan giants thrust four and five miles into the turbulent sky, creating a land of tectonic power and otherworldly dimensions.

It is here also that one finds the dramatic wedge of Ama Dablam (22,494′), considered the most beautiful peak in Nepal. Often compared to the Matterhorn, Ama Dablam is centered among a cluster of 22,000–24,000-foot peaks that surround the high valleys of the Sherpas, the people whose villages and hamlets dot the landscape. But not only is Ama Dablam 8,000 feet taller than its Swiss likeness, its steep glacier-encrusted walls and sharp, exposed ridges offer no easy route to the summit, as does the east ridge of the Matterhorn.

Ama Dablam (the name means "Mother's charm box" in the Sherpa language and refers to the large ice bulges high on the peak that resemble the traditional charm boxes Sherpa women wear around their necks) is located off the main Himalayan axis just south of Everest. The peak is surrounded by four other giants: Baruntse (23,688′), Chamlang (24,187′)—both of which are east of Ama Dablam and not visible from the valleys of the Khumbu—Kangtega (22,340′), and Thamserku (21,680′), spectacular ice-fluted sentinels to the southwest.

Ama Dablam, Khumbu, Nepal

After Nepal opened her doors to foreigners in 1950, the first Europeans to visit Khumbu and see this incredibly beautiful mountain were Bill Tilman and Charles Houston. A full-scale attempt on the north ridge was carried out nine years later but ended in disaster when Mike Harris and George Fraser disappeared near the summit. Then, in 1960, a long-term scientific and mountaineering expedition led by Sir Edmund Hillary arrived in the Khumbu region for a nine-month sojourn with a mandate to carry out physiological studies on man's ability to acclimatize at higher altitudes, to collect scientific data on glaciology, biology, and meterology, to look for the Abominable Snowman (or Yeti), and to climb Makalu (27,825′), the fifth-highest mountain in the world, without using oxygen. An additional goal was to winter a group of climbers-scientists high up on some Himalayan peak to carry out research in an Antarctic-type environment. A prefabricated hut was erected at 19,000 feet near the Mingbo La, a 19,080-foot pass leading from the Mingbo Valley to a high, glaciated valley east of Ama Dablam, known as the Hongu. After spending the winter of 1960–61 here, a party of four, Mike Gill, Barry Bishop, Mike Ward, and Wally Romanes, made the first ascent of Ama Dablam in March of 1961, after a continuous and difficult effort that lasted nearly a month, climbing the southwest ridge and the final, perfectly formed 800-foot ice flutings of the summit cone.

The popular approach route to Ama Dablam and the Khumbu region is presently by air from Kathmandu to the small airstrip of Lukla (9,240′), built by Sir Edmund on a grassy shelf above the Dudh Kosi River gorge. Others prefer the traditional expedition trail from near Kathmandu, a 180-mile trek that explores the contrasting middle hills of Nepal with their distinctly different tribal villages, elaborate terracing, and, on occasion, thick rhododendron forests. Eventually the Dudh Kosi

Tamserku Peak,
Khumbu

River is reached, where the trail merges with the track coming down from Lukla and proceeds to Namche Bazaar (11,300′). Namche is a prosperous market town and the cultural center of the Sherpa people who inhabit the Khumbu. Here also the icy summits of Thamserku, Kwangde (20,417′), and Khumbilha (18,720′), the sacred mountain of the Sherpas, tower above, while to the south endless ridges disappear into the haze of the Indian plains. Beyond Namche the terrain steepens considerably, and eventually one reaches the lamasery of Thyangboche (12,760′), where pine, azalea, and rhododendron surround a pagoda-like temple, framed by the world's most spectacular mountain scene: the peaks of Khumbu dominated not by Everest—which from here appears small and insignificant behind the large Nuptse wall—but of the much closer and dominant blunt obelisk of Ama Dablam, guarding the entrance to the Mingbo Valley and access to the upper reaches of the mountain's ridges and passes.

Amid this most majestic of the world's natural mountain amphitheaters live the hardy Sherpas, the legendary "people of the East," who migrated from Tibet and settled in these high southern valleys of the Himalaya over 100 years ago. Active Buddhists, they have built a fine culture of their own, patterned after the Mahayana Buddhism of Tibet. Friendly, cheerful, and accustomed to travel across the high passes on trading missions to Tibet, the Sherpas have become exceptional mountain guides as well as high-altitude expedition porters, distinguishing themselves on countless expeditions and often reaching important summits. Following Sir Edmund Hillary and Sherpa Tenzing Norgay's first ascent of Everest in 1953, Khumbu and the Sherpas have become world-famous, and today the Khumbu is the premier area for trekking in Asia.

During the past decade or so, Ama Dablam has become increasingly popular with hard-core mountaineers, as well as with organized climbing groups. Peter Hillary's (Sir Edmund's son) attempt in 1979 of the unclimbed west face ended in disaster when a huge avalanche swept one member of the party to his death while injuring Peter and his two other companions. The same year also saw the bold one-day solo climb of the formidable southface by Jeff Lowe, one of America's outstanding alpinists. Americans Hooman Aprin, Randall Harrington, and Martin Zabaleta climbed the southeast ridge in 1985, while in the same year an international expedition organized by Renato Moro managed to haul 13 people to the summit. Yet Ama Dablam remains a steep, dangerous, and difficult mountain for anyone bold enough to contemplate it, with chances for success largely dependent not on man's skill and perseverance, but on good conditions, which are the whims of the Himalayan gods.

Chain suspension bridge, Khumbu

Ningchin Kansha

South Tibet, China

While most of the world's mountain ranges—especially those with peaks over 20,000 feet—are well-charted and named, there remain (mainly in the vast and remote regions of northern Tibet) substantial masses of peaks that are still largely unexplored and unknown. Among these mountains of mystery is an unnamed 100-mile mountain ridge of high snow peaks that snakes north from Chomolhari, the sacred mountain of the Tibetans, on the Tibet/Bhutan border.

This little-known Himalayan spur comes to an end with Ningchin Kansha (23,593′), a peak first sighted in 1904 by the British military expedition under Colonel Francis Younghusband on its approach to Lhasa. Starting from near Darjeeling, the British fought their way into Tibet by first taking the city of Gyantse and the Gyantse Fort, then continued east, crossing the 16,800-foot Karo La just south of Ningchin Kansha, and entered Lhasa, the Holy and Forbidden City of Tibet, after ferrying their troops across the mighty Yarlung Tsangpo River.

Ningchin Kansha and the Karo La eventually became landmarks on the trade route between Kalimpong and Lhasa, established following a treaty signed in Lhasa by Colonel Younghusband. Yet for more than 80 years no attempts were made to climb this 23,000-foot giant so close to the road. The first serious attempt was made in 1985 by a team from Japan, but they were stopped at 21,600 feet on the southwest ridge. The mountain finally was scaled in 1986 by a team from the Tibetan Mountaineering Association, and the summit was reached after establishing camps at 20,000 feet and 22,600 feet. No less than 12 climbers made the top, including three Tibetans, Sang Zhu, Pemba, and Jia Bu.

Yaks grazing below Ningchin Kansha

Aside from dividing Tibet geographically, these mountains also cause cultural barriers to be raised, similar in a way to those that exist in the Alps to this day, with villagers of one large alpine valley showing prejudice toward a neighboring village across the mountain. In Tibet, the mountain walls, of which the Ningchin Kansha is a part, may have contributed to isolationism between the two dominant sects, commonly known as the Red Hats and the Yellow Hats. The history of Tibet is filled with quarrels and intrigue between these two powerful groups, headed by the Dalai Lama in Lhasa (who prior to his escape from the Communist Chinese invasion of Tibet was the spiritual head of the Red Hats—the Kagyupa sect) and the Tashi—or Panchen—Lama, the head of the Gelugpa sect, which hails from Shigatse, Tibet's second largest city, located west of the Ningchin Kansha Range.

After a quarrel broke out between the Lamas in 1923, the Tashi Lama fled to Beijing, seeking sanctuary with the Chinese. He remained there well past the death of the 13th Dalai Lama in 1933, causing the British to send a political mission to Lhasa in 1936 to help the Regent solve the problem of governing the political life of the country. Prior to these events, the Dalai Lama had fled the British in 1903, seeking refuge in Mongolia. He returned in 1909 but was forced to flee once again a short time later when 2,000 Chinese troops arrived in Lhasa. After a three-year absence from India (the British had since been befriended), he returned in 1912 following the Manchu revolution, and Tibet once again became an autonomous state. The Panchen

Ningchin Kansha

Lama meanwhile remained in Shigatse, secure in his huge Tashilumpo Monastery, built in the 15th century by the successor of Tsong Khapa, the founder of the Yellow Hat sect, together with an entourage of over 3,000 monks.

Nine years after the Communist takeover in 1950, the Dalai Lama had to flee

Tashilumpo Monastery, Shigatse

Tibet again, leaving the Panchen Lama (at least in the eyes of his Chinese overlords) once again in control of Buddhist affairs. To this day, the occupation of Tibet, and the ongoing fighting over that country's independence, remains one of the world's most tragic and unsolved conflicts.

Chomolhari

Eastern Himalaya, Bhutan/China

Majestic when seen from afar on the Tibetan plateau, Chomolhari looms nearly 10,000 feet above the barren plains of the Chumbi Valley. A border peak on the main Himalayan crest between Tibet and Bhutan, Chomolhari (23,977′) is a sacred mountain revered by all Buddhists as the goddess Chomo. The mountain is also the focal point for popular treks in western Bhutan, which begin from the town of Paro, and a prized climbing destination for mountaineers. The first ascent of this formidable peak was made by a small party consisting of Spencer Chapman and his Sherpa, Pasang Dawa Lama in 1937, along the south ridge. Chapman, who described his adventure (and misadventure) on Chomolhari in his book *From Helvellyn to Himalaya*, wrote of his unbelievable escape from death, falling off the summit (!) after having reached the top with his Sherpa companion. According to Chapman, he was standing on the summit taking photographs of Tibet when Pasang accidentally fell backward off the mountain and, being tied to Chapman with the climbing rope, pulled him along. Hurtling down toward the edge of the 10,000-foot southwest face, Chapman managed to drive his ice axe into the snow and arrest their slide in the nick of time. They lost most of their gear, including food, equipment, and a stove, and their descent into civilization became a five-day epic of survivial.

To the Bhutanese, Chomolhari is more than a mountain. It is a symbol of their Buddhist faith, which permeates their entire social structure as well as their cultural and religious life. Bhutan as a country was never conquered or colonized and remained until 1907 a theocracy ruled by the Drukpa Kagyupa sect of Buddhism, under a spiritual leader called the Dharma Raja (similar to the Dalai Lama of Tibet). Whereas other small Himalayan kingdoms have been absorbed or annexed by their larger neighbors—Hunza into Pakistan, Sikkim into India—Bhutan (like Nepal) has retained not only its independence but also its cultural heritage. Bhutan today is a hereditary monarchy, ruled by young King Jigme Wangchuk and a council of ministers.

Chomolhari and ruined dzong

In Bhutan the Buddhist culture and religion are everywhere in evidence—in the large *dzongs* (monastic forts) that dominate the cities of Paro, Thimpu, Punakha, and others; in the national dress worn by most Bhutanese; and by the fluttering prayer flags that adorn virtually every house in the kingdom. The monasteries are active and fully staffed with monks and apprentices who are being taught the ancient Buddhist scriptures and the art of blowing the eight-foot-long *radung* (horns), among other skills. In Thimpu, the capital, the Tashicho Dzong, the largest temple-monastery complex in Bhutan (and perhaps the largest in the Buddhist world) also serves as the seat of government and as palace for the king.

In terms of climbing and adventure tourism, Bhutan is not an open country like Nepal or India, where one can travel according to one's desire and pocketbook. Permits for travel in the interior must be secured in advance, and payment must be made for all travel arrangements, including food, porters, lodgings, pack animals, etc., to the Bhutanese authorities before one's arrival—at a predetermined rate set by the Bhutanese government. One is also obliged to take along a government guide for the duration of the trek or climb. It therefore comes as no surprise that climbing and

trekking expeditions in Bhutan have limited appeal, although the country is certainly not lacking in unclimbed peaks to be conquered or uncharted trekking routes to be established across a very colorful, charming, and fascinating landscape.

Among the highest peaks in Bhutan, aside from Chomolhari, are the unclimbed Kanker Punzum (24,740′), which was attempted by Japanese parties several years ago, and the icy pyramid of Kula Kangri (24,783′), which rises slightly north of the main Himalayan crest and has recently been marked on Chinese maps as lying completely within Tibet. This peak, long believed to be the highest in Bhutan, was climbed from the Tibetan side in 1986 by a Japanese expedition from Kobe University with a permit from the Chinese Mountaineering Association. It thus appears that Kanker Punzum is the reigning monarch of the Bhutan Himalaya—and as yet is unclimbed.

Opposite:
Taksang Monastery,
Bhutan

Young monks
in Thimpu,
Bhutan

The approach to Chomolhari can presently be made only from the Bhutanese side, the Tibetan Chumbi Valley being closed to all traffic from India by the Chinese authorities. Travel is by road or air to Paro or Thimpu, then on foot to the base camp of Chomolhari, a three-day trek. A number of interesting trekking options exist: one can head for Lingshi Dzong, a fine fort near the Tibetan border, or go further east to the hidden valleys of Lunana. Whatever one's choice, whatever the purpose or eventual destination, Bhutan and Chomolhari deserve a high rating on anyone's agenda for a superb Asian mountain experience.

EQUIPMENT FOR MOUNTAIN TRAVEL

BASIC EQUIPMENT

It is important to be properly equipped when traveling into the mountains. Warm clothes (using the layering system), raingear that works, appropriate boots for the terrain, pack, sleeping bag, etc., are all vital components of equipment for an enjoyable and successful outing into the high ranges of the world.

Remember, though, that equipment is not a substitute for experience, although better and safer equipment is enabling more and more mountain enthusiasts to pursue their objectives with a wider margin of comfort and ease.

There has been a virtual revolution in outdoor equipment during the past decade, not only in the basic concept of weight versus warmth, but also in variety and choice of available merchandise. Some of the more notable changes center around frameless packs, plastic hiking boots, and other synthetic items such as pile garments, Goretex raingear, and fiberfill.

Some of the major items on any outdoorman's list are his sleeping bag, boots, and pack. These are the essentials to keeping warm and dry in a variety of weather conditions. The following brief account will help explain some of the features and improvements in these basic items of equipment.

Sleeping bag. Your bag is one of the most important items you'll bring. After selecting a quality brand, your major choice concerns the type of fill. Down is very light, easily compressible, and thermally efficient when it is dry. It is also very expensive. Synthetic material known as fiberfill is not as compressible as down, but it's almost as light. Moreover, it's far less expensive. Although fiberfill is not as thermally efficient as down, it has one major advantage: it will keep you warm even when wet. Synthetics are thus preferable when camping out in wet climates, such as Alaska or New Zealand.

The temperature ratings that manufacturers give their sleeping bags are necessarily subjective. If you are in doubt about which bag to buy, get the one with the lower rating—you can always unzip the bag if it's too hot. For some trips, I recommend taking a cotton liner to be used as a substitute for the bag while you're traveling in hot lowlands.

Boots. What type of footgear to wear on a climbing trip? In a utopian world where weight and bulk didn't matter, one might like to have four or five pairs of shoes in order to constantly change them under differing conditions. Alas, footwear is bulky and heavy, and one must compromise. For many a hike or minor climb, a pair of light hiking boots will be the perfect choice. Waterproofed leather boots work well in snow or wet climates; lightweight boots that use Goretex (Nike, New Balance, etc.) are extremely comfortable and often adequate. Both types of boots can also be used in cities and on buses, as well as on the trails and higher up. Make sure your boots are in good condition and broken in before your trip.

Heavier boots are recommended for serious climbs and treks above 15,000 feet. If double plastic mountain boots are taken, be aware that they are unsuitable for general hiking. Once on the glacier or the mountain, they usually work fine.

There's still more to consider when talking about the lower extremities. Your choice of socks is a personal one; most people prefer hiking with a light pair, cotton or synthetic, next to the skin and a heavier pair, of wool or pile, over that. Gaiters, coverings that prevent snow or scree from entering your boots, are needed for cross-country hikes in rough terrain and general mountaineering purposes.

Packs. When a mountain trip calls for a large-sized pack, you should consider an internal-frame pack. These high-tech packs can be adjusted to hug the body like a garment and are especially appropriate in rugged country or on a cross-country ski mountaineering trip.

When considering a smaller pack, such as a daypack, check to see that it is made with tough fabric and has padded shoulder straps and a waist belt. Outside pockets are convenient for carrying water bottles and frequently needed items. A daypack can be used to carry bulky jackets and camera gear, and is excellent as a carry-on bag on a flight.

Insulated clothing. Both down and synthetic materials are used to make insulated clothing such as hats, jackets, pants, and booties. As a fill, down is expensive, light, compressible, and, when dry, thermally efficient. The less expensive synthetics have been greatly improved in the past few years, and more and more people are using them. Fabrics known as pile, bunting, Synchilla, Armadilla, and others, made from polyester pile fibers, are excellent insulators that refuse to absorb water (a distinct advantage in wet climates).

Layering. A climbing trip can be cold! Not arctic weather, perhaps, but chilly enough that to be comfortable you should have lightweight, sophisticated clothing and adhere to the "layering-system" approach to dressing. Next to the skin you should wear an undershirt of polypropylene or its equivalent; this will wick moisture from the skin to help keep you dry. The next layers are the ones that keep you warm: first a shirt, then a wool sweater, a light down jacket, or a pile jacket. An outer layer composed of a waterproof, windproof shell completes the picture for the upper body. You should follow the same principle for the lower body: polypropylene underwear, wool or pile pants, and windpants. Don't forget the extremities: you should wear gloves or mittens and a wool or pile hat—a surprising amount of heat escapes through the scalp.

REGIONAL SUGGESTIONS

Now for some specific suggestions regarding what to bring when traveling to any of the major mountain areas described in this book. Keep in mind that there are some basic differences between climbing in the Alps of Italy versus climbing in the Atlas of Morocco or in the Karakoram of China. The following comments will guide you in selecting the right gear for the destination of your choice.

North America. The traditional approach to the North American mountains is by backpacking, a time-honored style of traveling whereby one carries everything one needs. That includes tent, food, and fuel. Hut systems as in the Alps have by and large not taken hold in the United States and Canada, although occasionally new huts are being built. Camping is the accepted method. Equipment varies greatly with the region and the trek or climb that is being contemplated. In general, a sleeping bag and foam pad are essentials, as are a good, lightweight mountain stove, freeze-dried food, a lightweight tent, and raingear as the need may dictate. Lightweight hiking boots are fine for most mountain walks in North America where snow is not present. Special rock-climbing shoes are needed for climbing in Yosemite. Down gear is normally not needed.

South America. While the peaks are not as high or remote as in Asia, many parts of the Andes are still quite undeveloped and require a full complement of gear. Some regions are more advanced, however, such as the Cordillera Blanca, a prime climbing and trekking region in northern Peru, where an existing mountaineering infrastructure is thriving. In Huaraz, the capital of the region, one can purchase used mountain gear and hire guides as well. This also applies to Cuzco in central Peru. In Chile and Argentina the weather varies greatly—from hot in the northern deserts of Atacama to frigidly windy in Patagonia and the Towers of Paine. For the latter, a full complement of equipment is necessary, similar to what one would take to the Himalaya, except the temperatures are warmer. The central Andes are generally dry and stable during the months of May to September; the high peaks can be cold, however, and this must be taken into account for such giants as Aconcagua.

Europe. Since the weather is generally less reliable in the European Alps, people have come to rely not so much on quality raingear as on staying out of the rain altogether. Mountain huts are very popular in Europe and can be found on almost any alp or mountainside. There are well over 1,000 mountain huts in the western countries of France, Italy, Switzerland, Germany, and Austria, all of which provide shelter and overnight accommodations. One normally does not bring a sleeping bag on climbs in the Alps, unless long and difficult routes are planned with open bivouacs. Personal clothing consists of what one wears, with a spare set or two back at the hotel or hut. A medium pack usually suffices. Raingear is essential and must be of top quality.

Africa. The mountains of the Atlas and the Sahara are generally very dry and hot, requiring light cotton clothing, shorts, sun hat, and, of course, a full complement of camping equipment. For Kilimanjaro and Mt. Kenya climbs, extra warm clothes are needed because of the high altitudes that are attained on these mountains. A large pack is recommended for the big peaks, unless one hires porters.

Asia. The mountains are usually a long way from the nearest road or civilization, and the one-day approach of the Alps is not applicable in Asia. The march in, or "trek," is often the main ingredient of the climb of a minor peak. Trekking peaks are popular and in demand in places such as Nepal and India, with prospective mountaineers spending a great deal of time and care preparing and selecting their equipment for long weeks on the trail and among the high crags and snow slopes of the Himalaya and Karakoram. An extra-large pack, oversize sleeping bag (to keep your boots warm in the bottom during the night), plastic boots, a durable foam pad and quality tents are essential requirements for prolonged high-altitude treks and climbs in Asia.

MASTER EQUIPMENT LIST

The following is a master list that covers the full spectrum of clothing and equipment likely to be needed on any mountain journey in the world. The goal of the list is to present a complete selection of what is available today. Quantities have not been included. Use your judgment, keeping in mind the potential weather conditions and overall packing and weight restrictions for your trip.

Shirt
Wool or chamois, long-sleeved
Cotton, long-sleeved (buttoned front or turtleneck)
Cotton, short-sleeved (buttoned front or T-shirt)
Windshirt

Sweater
Heavy wool sweater
Pile jacket or light sweater

Trousers
Full-length (wool or blend, or pile)
Windpants of Goretex with side-leg zipper
Hiking shorts
Note: Some women prefer to hike in loose-fitting, calf-length skirts.

Underwear
Thermal, light-weight, top and bottom (polypropylene)
Thermal, medium-weight, top and bottom (polypropylene)
Thermal, heavy-weight, top and bottom (polypropylene)

Headwear
Silk or nylon face mask
Bandanna
Wool or pile hat (balaclava)
Light sun hat, with a wide brim
Ski cap

Insulated clothing
Expedition parka with hood (parka should contain 16-18 oz. of down or 20-26 oz. of fiberfill, and must fit over bulky clothing)
Medium-weight parka (10-12 oz. of down; 16-20 oz. of fiberfill)
Down or fiberfill vest
Down or fiberfill overpants
Warm-up pants or quilted underwear
Goretex climbing suit with bib overalls

Foul-weather gear
Goretex parka—or cagoule, anorak, or mountain parka—for rain and wind (must fit over bulky clothing)
Poncho (lightweight and sturdy)
Umbrella (lightweight and collapsible)
Rain cover for backpack
Traditional nautical foul-weather gear (waterproof rain suit, including parka, pants, and hat)
Rainpants

Handwear
Silk or nylon glove liners
Wool mittens (or pile or polypropylene)
Cotton garden gloves (for sun/wind protection)
Expedition overmitts (must fit over gloves)
Windproof and waterproof overmitts (must fit over gloves)

Socks
Heavy-duty (wool or pile)
Athletic type (cotton or synthetic)
Vapor-barrier socks

Footwear
Rock-climbing shoes
Light hiking boots, with padded ankle and lug sole
Medium-weight hiking boots
Heavy mountaineering boots
Plastic double boots
Down or fiberfill booties
Rubber thongs (for camp use and showers)

Gaiters and overboots
Insulated overboots with rugged bottoms (for use with heavy mountaineering boots)
Ankle gaiters
Knee-length gaiters
Supergaiters

Sleeping gear
Expedition-weight sleeping bag (with temperature rating of -10° F. to -25° F.)
Medium-weight sleeping bag (with temperature rating of 0° F. to 15° F.)
Light-weight sleeping bag (with temperature rating of 20° F. to 30° F.)
Cotton liner (no sleeping bag needed)

Pads
Open-cell foam, 3/4 length or full length, 2″ thick, with waterproof cover (not recommended for cold-weather use or on water-oriented trips)
Closed-cell type, 3/4 length, 3/8″ thick
Closed-cell type, 3/4 length, 3/4″ thick
Therma-Rest, 3/4 or full length

Ground sheet (lightweight but tough, 6′ by 8′)

Climbing equipment
Ice-axe (70-90 cm, depending on your height; metal or fiberglass shaft recommended, as is a sling for wrist or body attachment)
Crampons (12-point hinged, not rigid, and fitted perfectly to your boots or overboots)
Carabiners (one locking and two regular)
Two prusik loops, each made from a 12′ length of 5- or 6-mm perlon
Adjustable seat/chest harness
Helmet
Climbing rope—nylon, 9 or 11 mm, 120-150 feet

Packs, rucksacks, duffels
Expedition-type frame pack, with aluminum frame, padded hip belt, and roomy outside pockets. Capacity should be around 4,500 cu. in.
Medium-size frame pack with outside pockets and a capacity of about 3,800 cu. in.
Large internal-frame rucksack with capacity of about 4,500 cu. in.
Medium-sized internal-frame pack with capacity of about 3,500 cu. in.
Daypack, with capacity of about 1,500 to 2,000 cu. in.
Small daypack, with capacity of about 1,000 to 1,500 cu. in.
Duffel bag, sturdy and waterproof (medium: about 12″ by 30″ or large: about 15″ by 33″)
Buckled straps (or a hank of parachute cord)
Belt pack

Eating utensils
Cup and bowl (of heavy-duty plastic)
Spoon and fork
Pocketknife, preferably with can opener and scissors (Swiss Army type)
Water bottle, plastic and leakproof, 1- or 1.5-qt. capacity.

Accessories
First-aid kit, including any prescription medications
Toilet kit (soap, toothbrush, toilet articles)
Towelettes (disposable type like Wash 'N' Dry; for hygiene)
Toilet paper (one roll per camping week)
Insect repellent
Repair kit containing needle, thread, 1/8″ nylon cord, ripstop repair tape, safety pins, etc.
Sunglasses
High-altitude sunglasses or goggles, with extra-dark lenses (85% absorbency of visible light)
Spare eyeglasses or contacts (if you wear prescription lenses)
Glacier cream or zinc oxide (to screen ultraviolet rays)
Sun-blocking lotion
Sun-blocking lipstick or ointment
Flashlight (with spare batteries and bulb)
Head lamp (lightweight; with spare batteries and bulb)
Butane lighters (one or two)
Matches (waterproof and windproof)
Whistle (plastic coaches' type)
Compass (light, simple, and of good quality)
Topographical maps
Waterproof boot sealer (e.g., Sno-Seal)
Small, lockable suitcase for city clothes (unsuitable for trekking; can be stored in hotel while on the trail)
Stuff bags (assorted sizes and colors)
Plastic bags (various sizes)
Towel and swimsuit

Optional accessories
Camera, lenses, film, and tripod (with spare batteries)
Film shield (lead shield bag to carry film and/or camera, for X-ray protection)
Binoculars
Candle lantern and/or candles
Alarm watch
Reading and writing material
Fishing tackle (if appropriate)

Questions? If you desire further information about any of the equipment listed above, consult a specialist in a quality sporting-goods shop catering to hikers, campers, and mountain climbers. Or you may contact Mountain Travel, the Adventure Company, for a list of nationwide equipment suppliers that carry many of the items on this master list. Mountain Travel will also be happy to send you a copy of their current catalog of treks, outings, and expeditions, with a listing of more than 300 adventurous trips around the world, including trekking and mountaineering trips to most of the mountains illustrated in this book. (Mountain Travel, 6420 Fairmount Avenue, El Cerrito, CA 94530, (800) 227-2384)

Packing suggestions. I recommend that you hand carry onto the plane, boat, or bus (using a daypack is a great idea) your boots, camera, important documents, medicines, and other irreplaceable items. If your checked luggage includes a rucksack or a duffel bag, make sure small items within cannot escape. Attach baggage tags to each piece of luggage; it is also a good idea to add identification *inside* each piece.

A sturdy, waterproof duffel bag, with a full-length zipper and wraparound straps, is highly recommended for carrying the bulk of your gear. To discourage pilferage, use a combination-type lock to secure the zipper to the bag. A suitcase is not practical for use while on a trek or expedition.

Buckled straps are helpful for lashing gear onto the outside of your pack. Stuff bags are good for keeping gear dry and organized. Finally, bring a heavy-duty, garbage-can-sized plastic bag (to cover your pack in the rain) and a few sturdy plastic bags for film, books, and small items. Clear plastic Ziplock bags make it easy to see what you have plus protect your gear at the same time.

CHRONOLOGICAL LIST OF FIRST ASCENTS

Mountain	Country	Year	Party
Mt. Sinai 7,497′	Egypt	B.C.	Prophet Moses
Licancábur 19,455′	Chile	Prior to 1500	Atacameños Indians
Mont Blanc 15,771′	Italy/France	1786	Jacques Balmat and Michel Paccard
Ararat 16,946′	Turkey	1829	Dr. Friedrich Parrot and party
Mt. Elbrus (east peak) 18,481′	USSR	1829	Kilar Hashirov and Akia Sottaev
Mt. Shasta 14,162′	USA	1854	E. D. Pearce
Matterhorn 14,688′	Switzerland/Italy	1865	Edward Whymper and party
Tre Cime di Lavaredo 9,840′	Italy	1869	Paul Grohmann
Half Dome 8,842′	USA	1875	George Anderson
Kilimanjaro 19,340′	Tanzania	1889	Hans Meyer
Aconcagua 22,831′	Argentina	1897	Matthias Zurbriggen
Mt. Assiniboine 11,870′	Canada	1901	Sir James Outram
Huascarán (north peak) 21,833′	Peru	1908	Annie Peck
Gulmuthang 20,570′	India	1913	Mario Piacenza
Jbel Toubkal 13,671′	Morocco	1923	Marquis de Segonzac
Minya Konka 24,790′	China	1932	Richard Burdsall and Terris Moore
Sia Kangri 24,350′	India/Pakistan	1934	Gunther and Hettie Dyhrenfurth and party
Chomolhari 23,977′	Bhutan/Tibet (China)	1937	Spencer Chapman and Pasang Dawa Lama
Tezouiaig (South) 8,888′	Algeria	1937	Eduard Beyschlag and Hans Ellner
Volcán Osorno 8,727′	Chile	1948	Jan Renous
Yerupajá 21,768′	Peru	1950	Dave Harrah and Jim Maxwell
Mt. Everest 29,028′	Nepal/Tibet (China)	1953	Sir Edmund Hillary and Tenzing Norgay
K2 28,250′	China/Pakistan	1954	Achille Compagnoni and Lino Lacedelli
Totem Pole approx. 500′	USA	1957	William Feuerer, Mark Powell, Don Wilson and Jerry Gallwas
Paine Grande 10,600′	Chile	1957	Guido Monzino, Jean Bich, Leonardo Carrel, Camillo Pellissier, Tony Gobbi and Pierino Pession
Ama Dablam 22,494′	Nepal	1961	Mike Ward, Barry Bishop, Mike Gill, and Wally Romanes
Shivling 21,467′	India	1974	Hukan Singh and Laxman Singh
Batura-Hunza 25,570′	Pakistan	1976	Dr. Alexander Schlee and party
Ningchin Kansha 23,593′	Tibet (China)	1986	Sang Zhu, Pemba, Jia Bu, and 9 others
Mt. Taylor 3,274′	Antarctica	?	Unknown

SELECTED BIBLIOGRAPHY

NORTH AMERICA

Mt. Assiniboine:

Boles, Glen W., et al. *The Rocky Mountains of Canada South.* New York: American Alpine Club, 1979. Climbing guide to the Canadian Rockies.

Outram, James. *In the Heart of the Canadian Rockies.* New York: Macmillan, 1905. First ascent of Assiniboine.

Mt. Shasta:

Brewer, William H. *Up and Down California in 1860–1864.* New Haven: Yale University Press, 1930. Early climbs and travels in California.

Half Dome:

Roper, Steve. *Climber's Guide to Yosemite Valley.* San Francisco: Sierra Club, 1971.

Rowell, Galen. *The Vertical World of Yosemite.* Berkeley: Wilderness Press, 1974. Essays and photos on climbing in California's Yosemite Valley.

Totem Pole:

Crampton, C. Gregory. *Standing Up Country.* New York: Alfred A. Knopf, 1965. The canyonlands of Arizona and Utah.

Peattie, Roderick, ed. *The Inverted Mountains.* New York: Vanguard Press, 1948. Fine writings on travel and exploration of the southwest canyons.

SOUTH AMERICA

Huascarán:

Kinzl, Hans, and Erwin Schneider. *Cordillera Blanca (Peru).* Innsbruck: Universitats-Verlag Wagner, 1950. Exploration and climbing.

Ricker, John F. *Yuraq Janka: Cordilleras Blanca and Rosko.* New York: American Alpine Club, 1981. Guide to Peruvian Andes; good maps.

Yerupajá:

Sack, John. *The Ascent of Yerupajá.* London: Jenkins, 1954.

Aconcagua:

Ferlet, Rene. *Aconcagua: South Face.* London: Constable, 1956. First ascent of the great south wall of Aconcagua.

FitzGerald, E. A. *The Highest Andes.* London: Methuen, 1899. First ascent of Aconcagua.

Licancábur:

Bowman, Isaiah. *Desert Trails of Atacama.* New York: American Geographic Society, 1924. Explorations in northern Chile.

Volcán Osorno:

Bradt, Hilary. *Backpacking in Chile & Argentina.* Boston: Bradt Enterprises, 1980. A practical guide.

Mt. Taylor:

Fuchs, Sir Vivian. *Of Ice and Men.* London: Anthony Nelson, 1982. Thirty years of British expeditions in Antarctica (1943–73).

Herbert, Wally. *A World of Men.* New York: Putnam, 1969. Exploration in Antarctica.

EUROPE

Mont Blanc:

Bonatti, Walter. *Magic of Mont Blanc.* London: Victor Gollancz Ltd, 1985. Picture book on the Mont Blanc range.

Unsworth, Walt. *Savage Snows.* London: Hodder & Stoughton, 1986. The complete story of Mont Blanc.

Matterhorn:

Lunn, Arnold. *Matterhorn Centenary.* Chicago: Rand McNally, 1965. One hundred years of Matterhorn history.

Whymper, Edward. *Scrambles Amongst the Alps in the Years 1860–69.* London: Murray, 1900. First ascent of the Matterhorn.

Tre Cime di Lavaredo:

Brailsford, J. *Dolomites East.* London: Alpine Club, 1970. Guidebook to the eastern Dolomites.

Frass, Herman. *Dolomites, Mountains of Magic.* Bolzano: Athesia Press, 1977. Picture book and text on discovery and conquest of the Dolomites.

Mt. Elbrus:

Dunsheath, Joyce. *Guest of the Soviets.* London: Constable, 1954. Climbs in the USSR, including Elbrus.

Pereira, Michael. *Across the Caucasus.* London: Geoffrey Bles, 1973. Travels in the Caucasus Mountains.

Ararat:

Navarra, Fernand. *The Forbidden Mountain.* London: McDonald, 1956. Six Frenchmen look for the ark and climb Ararat.

Parrot, Friedrich. *Journey to Ararat.* New York: Harper & Bros., 1859. First ascent of Ararat.

AFRICA

Jbel Toubkal:

Collomb, Robin G. *Atlas Mountains Morocco.* Goring, Reading, Berks: West Col, 1980. Practical guide to the Atlas.

Mt. Sinai:

Bernstein, Burton. *Sinai.* New York: Viking, 1979. Travels, history and politics of the Peninsula.

Hazelton, Lesley. *Where Mountains Roar*. New York: Holt, 1980. Travels in the Sinai and Negev deserts.

Hoggar Mountains:

Moorehouse, Geoffrey. *The Fearful Void*. New York: J. B. Lippincott, 1974. Six-months-solo trek from Mauritania to Tamanrasset.

Norwich, John J. *Sahara*. New York: Weybright & Talley, 1968. Two thousand miles by landrover across the Sahara; maps and photographs.

Kilimanjaro:

Allan, Iain. *Guide to Mt. Kenya and Kilimanjaro*. Nairobi: Mountain Club of Kenya, 1981.

Reader, John. *Kilimanjaro*. New York: Universe Books, 1982. Picture book on Kilimanjaro.

ASIA

Batura-Hunza:

Miller, Keith. *Continents in Collision*. London: George Philip, 1982. British Royal Geographical Society expedition to Western Karakoram.

K2:

Maraini, Fosco. *Karakoram*. New York: Viking, 1961. Expedition to Gasherbrum IV.

Ridgeway, Rick. *The Last Step*. Seattle: Mountaineers, 1980. The American ascent of K2.

Shipton, Eric. *Blank on the Map*. London: Hodder & Stoughton, 1938. Exploration of Karakoram and Aghil mountains.

Sia Kangri:

Longstaff, Tom. *This My Voyage*. New York: Charles Scribner's Sons, 1950. Explorations of eastern Karakoram and Siachen Glacier.

Venables, Stephen. *Painted Mountains*. Seattle: Mountaineers, 1987. Recent expeditions to eastern Karakoram.

Workman, Fanny B., and W. H. Workman. *Two Summers in the Ice-wilds of Eastern Karakoram*. London: Unwin, 1917. A classic on climbs and explorations of the Karakoram.

Gulmuthang:

Peissel, Michel. *Zanskar, the Hidden Kingdom*. New York: Dutton, 1979. Trek across the Himalaya into Zanskar.

Snellgrove, David, and Tadeusz Skorupski. *The Cultural Heritage of Ladakh*. Warminster: Aris & Phillips, 1980.

Shivling:

Boardman, Peter. *The Shining Mountain*. London: Hodder & Stoughton, 1978. Expedition to Garhwal.

Keay, John. *When Men and Mountains Meet*. London: John Murray, 1977. History of mountaineering in Himalayas.

Minya Konka:

Burdsall, Richard L., and Arthur B. Emmons, 3rd., et al. *Men Against the Clouds*. Seattle: Mountaineers, 1980 (revised edition). First ascent by Americans of Minya Konka.

Murphy, Joseph E. *Adventure Beyond the Clouds*. Minneapolis: Dillon Press, 1986. Account of second American ascent of Minya Konka in 1982.

Mt. Everest:

Hornbein, Thomas F. *Everest, the West Ridge*. Seattle: Mountaineers, 1980. First American ascent of Everest in 1963.

Sayre, Woodrow Wilson. *Four Against Everest*. Englewood Cliffs: Prentice-Hall, 1964. Expedition to Everest; by the President's grandson. Daring attempt by four amateur mountaineers to climb Mt. Everest.

Ama Dablam:

Hillary, Sir Edmund and Desmond Doig. *High in the Thin Cold Air*. Garden City: Doubleday, 1962. Scientific and climbing expedition to the Khumbu region and Ama Dablam.

Ningchin Kansha:

Chapman, F. Spencer. *Lhasa the Holy City*. London: Chatto & Windus, 1938. Travels and explorations in Tibet.

Hopkirk, Peter. *Trespassers On the Roof of the World*. London: John Murray, 1982. The race for Lhasa.

Chomolhari:

Chapman, F. Spencer. *Helvellyn to Himalaya*. London: Chatto & Windus, 1940. Climbs in the Himalayas—first ascent of Chomolhari.

GENERAL REFERENCE:

Antarctica: Great Stories from the Frozen Continent. Sydney: Reader's Digest, 1985. Comprehensive history of Antarctica.

Bartle, Jim. *Trails of the Cordillera Blanca and Huayhuash of Peru*, 1981.

Baume, Louis C. *Sivalaya*. Seattle: Mountaineers, 1979. Exploration of the 8,000-meter peaks of the Himalaya.

Cleare, John. *The World Guide to Mountains and Mountaineering*. New York: Mayflower, 1979. Illustrated reference guide.

Kelsey, Michael R. *Guide to the Worlds Mountains*. Springville, Utah: Kelsey Publishing Co., 1984. Contains descriptions of over 300 mountains and 377 maps.

Le Bon, Leo. *Where Mountains Live*. New York: Aperture, 1987. Twelve great treks, including Everest, K2, Kilimanjaro, and Paine.

Neate, Jill. *Mountaineering in the Andes*. London: Expedition Advisory Centre, 1987. Index to South American mountains.

Noyce, Wilfred, and Ian McMorrin, eds. *World Atlas of Mountaineering*. London: Macmillan, 1969.

Price, Larry W. *Mountains and Man*. Berkeley: University of California Press, 1981. Textbook on the ecology and geography of mountains.

Rowell, Galen. *Mountains of the Middle Kingdom*. San Francisco: Sierra Club Books, 1983. Mountain travel in China, illustrated.

Terray, Lionel. *Conquistadors of the Useless*. London: Victor Gollancz, 1963. Biography of a famous mountaineer.

GLOSSARY OF MOUNTAINEERING TERMS

Acclimatization: Adaptation of the body to higher altitudes.

Aiguille: French for "needle;" sharp, rock peak in the French Alps.

Alp: High mountain pasture, meadow.

Bivouac: Overnight in the outdoors without tent or other shelter.

Buttress: Wall of a cliff between two gullies.

Cairn: Stone marker indicating a trail or summit.

Col: Pass, low point between two peaks.

Cordillera: Mountain range (Spanish).

Cornice: Overhanging lip of hard snow along crest of ridge.

Couloir: Steep gully on a mountain side.

Crampons: Steel spikes strapped on climbing boots to aid in climbing snow or ice.

Crevasse: Crack or crevice in the surface of a glacier.

Eight-thousander: Colloquial for a peak over 8,000 meters high (the equivalent of 26,247 feet).

Gaiters: Canvas ankle wrappings to keep snow out of boots.

Glacier: Stream of ice, slowly descending a high mountain.

Glissade: Controlled slide down steep slopes of hard snow.

Gully: Gash or cleft in mountain side, not as long or steep as a couloir.

Hanging glacier: Glacier on a rock shelf high on a mountain.

Ice-axe: Mountaineer's tool to climb snow and ice.

Knife-edge: Narrow crest of rock on mountain ridge.

Leader: The first man on the rope, the guide.

Ledge: Usually a narrow, level space on a mountainside where one can sit or camp.

Moraine: Residual rock and debris left by a retreating glacier.

Pinnacle: Sharp point or tower of rock, smaller than aiguille.

Pitch: A rope length on a climb, a lead between two stances.

Piton: Metal spike nailed into a rock crevice to aid progress while climbing, also used for protection or anchor.

Quebrada: Narrow, U-shaped alpine valley (Spanish).

Rappell: Technique of sliding down a climbing rope.

Ravine: Steep and narrow valley or cleft surrounded by mountain walls.

Refuge: Mountain hut, cabin.

Ridge: A sharp corner of rock or ice where two faces or walls of a mountain meet.

Route finding: Searching for a way up a mountain.

Saddle: Wide, broad, low passage on a ridge between two peaks.

Scramble: Easy climb (non technical) on broken rock.

Scree: Loose stones, gravelly rock, which accumulates at the base of the mountain.

Snowline: Where snow remains year round on a mountain.

Spitze: German for "peak."

Traverse: Climbing along a mountain in a horizontal fashion.

ACKNOWLEDGMENTS

Gathering the photographs for *Majestic Mountains* has taken me on a total of 44 trips covering more than 30 countries in as many years. I would not have been able to accomplish this without the help and assistance from a great many people: from fellow travelers, mountaineers, editors, researchers, friends and family, and group sponsors.

The contributions of the following individuals and organizations have been of particular significance:

Travel: Alfredo Ferreyros, Nestor Morales, J.L. Bernezat, Wu Ming, Lanny Johnson, Peter Bruchhausen, Alla Schmitz, Ray Jewell, Sara Jacobson, Sir Edmund Hillary, Pepe Alarcon, Fikret Gurbuz, Gaston Oyarzun, Ramatullah Beek, Gustavo Giro.

*Climbing:*Mort Hempel, Gordon Wiltsie, Narendra Kumar, Jim Williams, Jerry Corr, Major Cherian, Allen Steck, Stan Armington, William and Suzanne Le Bon, Slava Voskovy, Omar of Imlil.

Editing, Research, and Design: Dena Bartolome and Steve Roper; Lois Brown and Dirk Luykx of Abrams.

Organizational Support: Chinese Mountaineering Association (Beijing), Himalayan Journeys (Kathmandu), Tropical Ice (Nairobi), Sovalpsport (Moscow), ExplorAndes (Lima), Trek Travel (Istanbul), Antartur (Ushuaia), Ace Turismo (Santiago), Hommes & Montagnes Du Sahara (Paris), Neot Hakikar (Jerusalem), Walji Travel (Islamabad), Mercury Himalayan Exploration (Delhi), Pan American (San Francisco), Lan Chile (Los Angeles), Air India (New York), Thai Airways (Seattle), British Airways (San Francisco), Pakistan International Airlines (New York), Ladeco (Los Angeles), Royal Air Maroc (Chicago), Indian Government Tourist Organization (New York), Government of Bhutan (Thimphu), Indian Army and Major General Saklani (Dehli), Hertz (San Francisco), Atlas Sahah Treks (Morocco).

And for her continued encouragement to complete the project: my wife, Nadia, a joyous companion on more than 10 of my expeditions.

To all, my grateful thanks.

Leo Le Bon